Your Financial Action
PLAN

Your Financial Action
PLAN

12 Simple Steps to Achieve Money Success

G. Cotter Cunningham

WILEY

John Wiley & Sons, Inc.

Published by John Wiley & Sons, Inc., Hoboken, New Jersey.
Published simultaneously in Canada.

For general information on our other products and services, or technical support, please contact our Customer Care Department within the United States at 800-762-2974, outside the United States at 317-572-3993 or fax 317-572-4002.

Wiley also publishes its books in a variety of electronic formats. Some content that appears in print may not be available in electronic books.

For more information about Wiley products, visit our web site at www.wiley.com.

ISBN 0-471-65030-7

Printed in the United States of America

10 9 8 7 6 5 4 3 2 1

CONTENTS

ACKNOWLEDGMENTS

This book is the culmination of the work of many people, and I am grateful to all of them. Special thanks go to:

- Literary agent Arthur Klebanoff, who truly guided this project to completion.
- To Elisabeth DeMarse and Bernice Kanner, who were the driving forces behind this effort.
- Publisher Joan O'Neil and the rest of the team at Wiley—Elke Villa, Felicia Reid, Michael Onorato and Peter Knapp—who saw the need for this type of book.
- Editors David Pugh and Debbie Englander, who were complete professionals and a pleasure to work with.
- All of my terrific colleagues at Bankrate, especially our editor in chief Dan Ray, our amazing financial analyst Greg McBride, CFA, and the always terrific Julie Bandy. Also assisting through out the process were Kay Bell, Dr. Don Taylor, CFA, Paula Sirois, Bob DeFranco, Karen Christie, and Pookie Skoran.
- Special thanks to Carol Holding, Janine Gordon, and Annie Weber, our Financial Literacy "dream team."
- Tom Evans and Peter Morse for giving me this opportunity.
- And finally, my family—I am the luckiest guy I know.

Cotter Cunningham
September, 2004

FOREWORD

When I became involved with Bankrate in 1993, managing one's finances effectively was difficult at best. The ability to obtain timely "apples to apples" comparisons of various banking products such as mortgages, CDs, credit cards, home equity and auto loans was limited mostly to rates published in newspapers and magazines. This information was usually provided by Bank Rate Monitor, our predecessor company. At that time, Bankrate covered only 16 products in just 25 markets. Although there were many options available to consumers, a comprehensive view of the best banking products and rates for their needs was all but impossible to obtain.

All that has changed. Today, Bankrate offers editorial and rate information on 250 products in more than 200 markets nationally—with products and markets being added constantly. Up-to-the-minute rate comparisons and product information are instantaneously available for free to the individual through Bankrate.com. Each year so many people consult Bankrate.com that it has become the leading consumer banking site on the Internet. Its rate information is distributed by 140 newspapers, including nine of the nation's top ten, a roster that includes such luminaries as the *Wall Street Journal*, *The New York Times,* and *USA Today*. Bankrate is even the data source of record for the Associated Press, Bloomberg Financial Markets, and the Federal Reserve.

In recent years, Bankrate has expanded beyond the rates arena to cover an increasingly broad array of consumer finance issues. We have added financial calculators, email newsletters, a weekly Rate Trend Index to help predict interest rate trends, and new channels on investing, taxes and small business.

There is a very high level of trust in the Bankrate brand thanks to its dedication to both high-quality journalism and rigorously checked rates data. Together, they allow consumers to become educated, make valid comparisons and then act with confidence. Today, five million Americans turn to Bankrate each month to help them with their most important financial decisions.

Our years of looking at consumer personal finance issues comprehensively and objectively come together in this book. We have distilled the most fundamental financial needs of consumers into an action plan. With its 12 easy steps, you can be in control of all your finances. I very much hope you will use them.

Peter C. Morse
Chairman, Bankrate, Inc.

introduction
THE HOLE IN YOUR POCKET

What Is Financial Literacy?
Where Does America Stand?

You may have academic smarts and street smarts, and may even be able to pick stocks more wisely than by throwing darts at a wall. If you are not financially literate, however, you are not really smart. A Ph.D. may not keep you out of the Poor House Door if you are not also committed to good personal finance habits.

Sad to say, most Americans are not. They are woefully unprepared, walking around the financial jungle with paper bags on their heads. By being uninterested, they are paying too much interest! They are very likely paying more than they should in fees—and earning less than they could in credits. And all those money concerns may be keeping them up at night.

A record number of Americans have mortgages now, and they turn to the business pages often before even checking out the headline news. Money has become, if not an obsession for many of us, then an overriding preoccupation—how to stretch it, make it, and use it.

Bankrate.com, the leading provider of personal finance information on the Internet, commissioned its first study on America's financial literacy in 2003, and repeated the same set of questions in 2004 to a nationally representative sample of 1,000 Americans. The survey employed the gold standard of polling—random-digit telephone dialing—and has a margin of error of three percent. We commissioned this study to find out how financially sophisticated Americans are so that we could make our Internet site, Bankrate.com, better and more useful to our readers.

We asked Americans if they pay bills on time to avoid late fees, read their bank statements regularly, check their credit reports annually for accuracy, have emergency funds of at least three months' living expenses, and have wills. We probed whether Americans shop around for the best insurance rates and coverage, comparison shop for the best deals on their mortgages, and look around for and switch to credit cards with lower rates. We questioned whether Americans follow monthly budgets, adjust their W-4s annually to make sure they are not giving the government too much money, and whether they contribute to retirement accounts.

When Bankrate released the findings of its benchmark "Financial Literacy" study in 2003 and again in 2004, it captured the interest of print, radio, and television outlets nationwide, all keen to report on the state of America's financial literacy. The seminal finding of the study is that most Americans are aware of what to do when it comes to managing their money. Americans are reasonably well-educated about the basics of money management. However, when Bankrate asked if people were actually doing these things, only 10 percent of our survey respondents got an "A." Most received a "D" or "F."

We have a gap between attitude and action. And it is this gap that contributes to Americans' anxieties about money. Twenty-four percent of Americans profess to be dissatisfied with their personal financial situations. Another 44 percent are only somewhat satisfied. Perhaps more revealing is that while three out of five people believe they are in control when dealing with their personal finances, that same number has neither refinanced their mortgages in the last few years, nor do they know how much life, auto, and health insurance to carry.

In *Your Financial Action Plan*, Bankrate.com, which collects and distributes information on more than 200 financial products, offers a 12-step self-analysis guide so readers can determine how financially literate they are. We then provide 12 simple steps to help people forge the financial futures they want.

Unlike other books in the money bin, *Your Financial Action Plan* is *not* about stocks and bonds and investments. It's about the gap between what you know and what you need to do in your day-to-day encounters in personal finance—a gap that is costing you money. Using Bankrate's expertise and easy-to-understand guides, closing this gap is not difficult. But the benefits are monumental.

In January 2004, Bankrate.com again commissioned RoperASW to survey 1,000 adult Americans about what they know about money matters and how well they manage their finances. Sad to say, our report card is not improving. With a grade of 66 out of 100, Americans get a "D" in the subject, almost flunking.

You may never have to translate Beaudelaire, determine the chemical composition of gases, or untangle the symbolism in *Alice in Wonderland* once you leave school. But you will always have to deal with money matters. And if you have poor habits and do not follow through on the basics, it can really hurt you.

What you know about financial matters really matters, not just for the more comfortable bottom line that invariably accompanies good habits, but because of the more comfortable sleep you will derive from peace of mind. Those who have a solid grasp of financial issues are richer in many ways. For example, financially literate people paid substantially less for their home loans than those with little financial literacy. Students at the top of the financial class locked in mortgages with a mean interest rate of 5.95 percent. Those at the bottom of the financial class ended up with loans carrying a 6.8 percent rate—a 14 percent difference amounting to thousands of dollars a year in saved interest expense.

Most Americans are laggards when it comes to financial fitness—and pay lavishly for their ignorance in their bottom lines and comfort. Where do you stand—or slide—on the issues? Take our 12-step self-analysis test to see if, financially speaking, you are in as sorry a state as much of the rest of the union. At the end, you can grade yourself. But remember, even if you in your finances resemble the overweight person who perpetually vows to start dieting next week, you *can* draw the line in the sand. Taking this self-assessment is the first step.

Get out a piece of paper and a pen. Then read each of the twelve questions carefully and rate yourself using the following scale:

If your response is...	*...give yourself this many points*
All the time	
(or Yes for questions 4, 6, and 10)	3
Sometimes	2
Rarely	1
Never	
(or No for Questions 4, 6, and 10)	0

1. Do you keep an emergency fund of at least three months' living expenses?
2. Do you regularly pay your bills on time?
3. Do you faithfully follow a monthly budget?

4. Did you contribute to either a company-sponsored retirement *5*
   account or an Individual Retirement Account (IRA) within
   your past working year?
5. How often do you read your bank account statements? *3.*
6. Have you prepared a will? *0*
7. How regularly do you shop around for the best insurance *2*
   quotes and coverage?
8. Do you regularly look for and switch to credit cards with *0*
   lower rates?
9. Do you check your credit report annually for accuracy? *0*
10. How regularly do you make more than the minimum pay- *3*
    ments on your credit cards? *5*
11. Do you comparison shop for the best deal on your mortgage? *1*
12. Do you adjust your W-4 form annually to make sure you are *0*
    not giving the government too much money?

How do you compare? Grade yourself.

Example	
Total points scored	28
Number of questions answered	12

Add up your total number of points. Divide by the number of questions you answered. Multiply the answer by 33.333 to convert your
score to a percentage score.

Grade yourself on a 100-point scale: 90–100 is an "A," 80–89 a
"B," 70–79 a "C," 60–69 a "D," and 59 and below an "F." In the
example given, 28/12 × 33.3333 = 77.78, or "C+".

Overall, Americans scored a "D" for financial literacy, which is no
better than in 2003. The grading curve broke down like this:

Score	Grade	% of Americans who "made the grade"*
90–99.99	A	7
80–89.99	B	19
70–79.99	C	20
60–69.99	D	19
0–59.99	F	36

*Adds to more than 100 due to rounding

What follows are eleven findings from the survey.

1. Two out of three people say it is very important to keep at least three months' living expenses in an emergency fund and another 26 percent consider it somewhat important. (After all, rainy days happen and people lose jobs and have car accidents.) Yet only 40 percent actually follow through on this ideal and another 28 percent do so only sporadically.

2. Although 93 percent of all Americans agree it is "very important" to pay bills on time to avoid late fees, only 80 percent claim to do it consistently. For some credit card companies, late payment penalty fees are an onerous $39, with the average late fee around $26.

3. People give budgeting lip service. They understand the value of a budget, but most do not make one. Nor do they track their expenses.

4. While most people acknowledge that they *should* regularly contribute to an individual retirement account (IRA), fewer than one in three is doing so regularly. If you are under age 50 and earned $3,000 in that year, you can deposit up to $3,000 annually in your IRA; those 50 and older can plunk in $3,500. Under tax legislation passed in 2001, the contribution amounts for individuals younger than 50 will increase incrementally

until hitting a $5,000 contribution level in 2008. Older workers also will be able to invest more in their IRAs each year, with the catch-up amount topping out at $1,000 in 2008. In a traditional IRA, that cache grows tax-free until it is withdrawn, usually after age 59½. Money withdrawn before age 59½ will usually get hit with a ten percent penalty, but there are some exceptions. In a Roth IRA, money invested will grow, and can be withdrawn in retirement, tax-free.

5. Seventy-four percent of people say they regularly read their bank account statements. Unfortunately, there are some people who are not even sure what type of account they have! An interest-bearing checking account, for example, usually requires you keep a minimum balance. A non–interest-bearing checking account may not require a minimum balance, but you earn zero interest on your deposits.

   Those who do not read their statements cannot sync them with their checks, recognize fees such as monthly service charges, or make sure they have sufficient funds to cover a check. Knowing when your checks are paid and deposits are available can prevent you from overdrawing your checking account and facing some nasty fees.

6. Despite the saying, "Where there's a will there's a way," more than 40 percent of people 35 and older do not have one. Where there's not a will, there's a way for a dispute to arise. People need wills to ensure that their assets go to whomever they choose.

7. Some 61 percent of Americans say it is very important to shop around for the best insurance quotes and coverage, but just 39 percent actually do it. (Amazingly, 59 percent admit they do not know how much life, auto, and health insurance they have—or should carry.) And when it comes to credit cards,

most Americans know that switching to one with a lower interest rate is a good idea, yet 31 percent never bother to do it. Indeed, 24 percent say that as long as they can afford their payments, they do not worry much about the interest rates they are paying. This is akin to tossing money out the window.

8. Whether you are applying for a loan or credit, knowing what your credit report says about you will determine not just whether you get the loan but how much you will pay for it. Yet while 44 percent believe that it is very important to check their credit report annually for accuracy, only 30 percent do it.

9. Almost three-quarters of Americans say they always make more than minimum payments on their credit cards. This is very good news. Now we just have to make it a habit to pay off the balance each month!

10. A fourth of those with mortgages did not comparison shop for them, despite the fact that a mortgage is the biggest single financial transaction most people make in their lifetimes.

11. Some 54 percent of Americans say it is very important to adjust their W-4 forms annually to make sure the correct amount is being withheld from their paychecks for income taxes, but just 38 percent do it.

Did you make the dean's list? Only a quarter of Americans did. More than a third failed the quiz. The reason is that most of us know what we should do when it comes to personal finances, but a lot of us do not do it. We tend to put off today the financial chores that we can do tomorrow.

A record 1.65 million consumers filed for bankruptcy in 2003. Many more are expected to take that drastic step in the next few years. Do not let yourself be one of them. Close the gap between what you know you should be doing financially and what in fact you are doing.

This book gives you useful facts you need to know to become a smart money manager. Our chapters are easy to follow, organized by the questions in the financial literacy quiz you just took. You can read the book straight through or focus only on the chapters that cover areas where you scored poorly. Either way, you will find valuable tools to help you take control of your finances.

While money may not actually buy happiness, knowing how to manage money effectively provides greater peace of mind. Overwhelmingly, those who are financially savvy are much more likely to be satisfied with the state of their personal finances and much more in control. When so much in life is out of our control, the reduced stress that financial literacy affords is, to borrow a MasterCard phrase, priceless. Let's put the "fun" back in *funds!*

Your Financial Action
PLAN

chapter one

RAINY DAY FUNDS AND SUNNY DAY SAVINGS

Prepare for an Emergency
Understand Asset Allocation
Build a Financial Plan

Do you keep an emergency fund? You can be fairly certain of three things in life: death, taxes, and rainy days. Accidents happen. Companies move or close. Illnesses strikes. Like they say about your computer's hard drive, it's not a question of *if* it will fail, but *when*.

People definitely know that having an emergency fund is important. In Bankrate's surveys, 93 percent agree it's necessary, with 71 percent of people saying it's very important to keep at least three months' living expenses on hand. Yet despite the likelihood that they will need to tap some cash to get through a rough patch, only 44 percent of Americans have established an emergency fund.

This is hardly their only monetary worry.

- 45 percent fear that they will not be able to put away enough money for retirement.

- 34 percent worry their employer will decrease their benefits.
- 33 percent fear they will lose their job.
- 32 percent lose sleep over real estate concerns, worried the value of their home will decrease.
- 30 percent worry they will not be able to pay their mortgages or rent.
- 29 percent fear they will not be able to pay their credit card bills.

When creating an emergency fund, the rule of thumb is to stow between three and six months' worth of income someplace where it earns interest until you need it. "Need" means that you're facing a financial sickness, not a mere hiccup. It does not mean that a piece of jazzy technology has suddenly caught your eye.

At Bankrate, we recommend starting with small steps. For example, saving just $50 each pay period (assuming biweekly pay) in a money market account will build to more than $2,600 in two years. The most important thing is to take the plunge: Pay yourself first and start saving.

An emergency fund should be part of your savings plan, but by no means the only part. After all, saving is not just about putting money aside: It's about collecting interest. Interest is what a borrower pays a lender for the use of the lender's money. This is what you get when you deposit money in a savings account: You lend that financial institution your money so it can make loans to someone else. For this privilege the bank or other financial institution pays you interest.

What is interesting about this are the terms "rate" and "yield." The rate is the stated interest rate on your investment—say, three percent on a certificate of deposit (CD). The annual percentage yield (APY) includes the effects of compounding and is determined by how often interest is paid.

Assume that your CD is invested at three percent APY for six months. You can figure out the interest by multiplying the amount invested by three percent and by the fraction of a year the money is invested, (in this case half a year). If a $10,000 investment pays interest semiannually you'll earn $150 interest. ($10,000 × 3 percent × ½ year.) The more often interest is paid, the higher the yield because the principal compounds and starts earning interest along with the invested principal. Got it? The annual percentage yield reflects the total interest to be earned based on an institution's compounding method, assuming funds remain in the account for a year.

So forget about the mattress or kitchen freezer. We may stow a few bills there, but when it comes to building *real* savings, you need to turn elsewhere. Here are some places to park the good (and, we hope, plenty) and still keep your finances liquid, meaning that they are easy to withdraw:

○ CDs are not just about beautiful music (though jumbo CDs do sound awfully sweet). They're certificates of deposit and they're safe enough for even the most risk-averse investor. The posted APYs let you compare CDs that mature the same day but will leave you with different-sized nest eggs. Some CDs come with bump-up clauses where the bank increases your rate on a predetermined agreement. Some let you cash in your CD before its maturity date, without penalty, to buy CDs that pay higher interest. Others come with flexible rates that allow you to make additional deposits and, occasionally, some withdrawals during the term of the CD. Be sure you know the terms of the CD before you buy it. Bankrate.com's "100 High" list provides the names, phone numbers, and rates of financial institutions that pay the highest rates in the United States. And Bankrate.com's "Safe and Sound" rating system assesses the financial health of 22,000 institutions, so you can check on the stability of any financial institution before making your deposit.

○ Financial advisers suggest "laddering" your investments. Take a CD ladder as an example. A CD ladder works in increments: Instead of buying one $50,000 CD, you buy a $10,000 one-year

CD, a $10,000 two-year CD, and so on, staggering them until your last $10,000 buys you a five-year CD and (hopefully) increases your rate of return. Consider each increment a rung on the ladder. After each increment (say, your one-year CD matures) you reach up to the next "rung"—reinvest that money in a five-year CD because by that time your five-year CD has four years left until it matures. As each year's CD comes due, you roll it into a five-year CD.

o Interest-bearing negotiable orders of withdrawal (or NOW accounts) are essentially interest-bearing checking accounts. Many let you "sweep" money from related accounts into them to take advantage of their higher yields.

o A Christmas Club is designed to let you set aside money for holidays or any special savings goal but it comes with a penalty for early withdrawals and often doesn't pay competitive rates.

o Annuities are regular, periodic payments made by an insurance company to a policyholder for a specified period. Fixed annuities provide a guaranteed return and grow tax-sheltered until you withdraw the money. But they're not the place to plunk your tax-advantaged retirement accounts such as 401(k) plans or Individual Retirement Accounts, (IRA) and they're not "emergency" money. If you withdraw your money from an annuity in the first six to eight years, you will pay a hefty surrender charge.

o Money market mutual funds invest in short-term corporate and government debt securities and earn a variable interest rate that is often comparable to the interest earned on CDs. You may withdraw money at any time without penalty.

o Credit unions have their own version of a savings account called a Share account. Their Share account certificates are like bank CDs and their share draft checking accounts are like a bank's checking account.

- A money market account (MMA) pays a higher interest rate than a standard savings account, usually requires a minimum balance, limits check writing and often charges a monthly service fee if the minimum balance is not maintained. The Federal Deposit Insurance Corporation (FDIC) insures these accounts.

- A passbook savings account is an interest-bearing savings account where the saver records transactions in a small book. Most banks have moved away from these accounts and substituted statement savings accounts, in which monthly statements replace the passbooks.

- Bonds are debt security, meaning you're lending money to a company or government that gives you essentially an IOU. Interest is paid either at specific periods during the life of the bond or when the bond matures. The principal or face value is repaid at maturity. If a bond with a $1,000 face value matures on December 31, 2006, for example, you will receive $1,000 on that date no matter what is happening in the market and as long as the issuer does not default on this obligation. Bonds issued by the United States Treasury are free from any risk of default.

- Savings bonds earn tax-deferred interest. You buy one at a deep discount compared to its face value. This discount is actually the interest that will accumulate during the life of the bond. A zero-coupon bond (also called a "zero") pays zero interest during the life of the bond, but pays the full face value on the bond's maturity date. Most people buy zeros issued by the U.S. government or state and local municipalities. Make sure your zero-coupon bond is noncallable—one that the issuer cannot make you redeem before the maturity date. Most Treasury and municipal zeros are noncallable. If you need to cash the bond prematurely, you may be stuck. You'll be selling it on the open market in competition with new bonds that may be cheaper.

If your assets were a pie, the biggest slice would probably be your home. Over a lifetime it's the No. 1 wealth builder for most Americans. But just where else you put your money depends a great deal on your personality and age—or how close you are to retiring. Historically, the stock market has been the best long-term investment vehicle. But in the short term, it's more of a roller-coaster ride. If your stomach lurches every time the Dow Jones Industrial average hiccups you probably should put more money into bonds or other less risky places. Know your emotional and numerical willingness for risk. Do not invest money in the stock market that you're not willing (or can't afford) to lose.

Once you have established a three-month emergency fund, you can give yourself a freedom fund—the freedom to walk out if your boss turns into a nerd or the company you spurned to go work for your current one acquires yours. At Bankrate, we cannot emphasize strongly enough the psychological benefit of a freedom fund, even if you never use it. Figure out what you would need to go six months without a job and build from there. Consider adding your income tax refund to your emergency fund; this will help bolster your savings from a three-months emergency fund to the full six-months "freedom fund" more quickly.

Start saving soon to take advantage of compounding. As Einstein famously said, compound interest is the most powerful force in the universe! The sooner you begin, the more money you'll have.

So an emergency fund is money you set apart from your portfolio and apart from assets you have allocated to various (and, hopefully wealth-building) investments. In addition to an emergency fund, you also need to save for retirement, for a down payment on a home, and for your children's education. When it comes to your long-term goals, asset allocation can be the difference between a really good portfolio and one that keeps you up at night. The right mix of stocks, bonds, cash, and alternative investments such as real estate, futures, and commodities can help you and your portfolio ride out the bad times intact.

In the financial arena, the letters IRA stand for Individual Retirement Account, and it is a great way to save for your future. Many workers may be eligible to set up a Roth IRA account which uses after-tax dollars. When you take money out in a qualified distribution, however, you pay no federal tax. A traditional IRA is funded with pre-tax dollars. You can open an IRA bank account, brokerage account, or mutual fund account and you can move the account around at will.

Taking advantage of your employer's 401(k) plan is also important for providing for your future financial security. In addition to accumulating tax-deferred assets, many companies will make contributions to your account if you do. This is free money! How often does that happen?

What should you invest in with your IRA or 401(k)? The most important factors to consider are how liquid is the investment, how long you will hold it, the expected return, inflation, and your risk tolerance.

For instance, if you have more than 15 years left in the workforce, some experts suggest putting as much as 75 percent of your capital in stocks, the rest in bonds, and none in cash. Depending on your comfort level, you can put more money in stable blue chip stocks and some money in risky technology stocks, and a high percentage of your government bonds in instruments with an intermediate time frame, say five to ten years. A stock portfolio should be diversified, or spread out according to the type of stock. Stocks are typically put in categories according to the size of the company and the relative value of the stock. There are Small-, Mid- and Large-Cap stocks. Cap is short for Market Capitalization, or the number of shares outstanding multiplied by the price of the stock. When you buy a stock at a certain price you are not only paying a price per share but all of the shares that everyone owns of a certain company added up equals the real price all of the investors are paying for the company. Next when you compare that market capitalization to the revenues, earnings, profitability, or book value of the company you see that you are either buying a company because it is growing, or a "growth" company, where you typically pay a high price. Or, you can buy "value" companies—companies selling for a price closer to what the company's assets are worth. And all of these categories can be either domestic or international companies that do business in long established markets like the United States and Europe, or "emerging" markets like China, Singapore and Chile. (One rule of thumb is that investors should expect about 8 percent average annual return on stocks and a 5 to 6 percent return on bonds, depending on inflation and the immediate past returns on stocks and bonds.) In general, experts agree that a well diversified portfolio provides the lowest volatility and the highest rate of return.

One big mistake many people make is looking at how an asset class did last year—and expecting a similar performance in the year ahead. Another is not reviewing their asset allocation at least once every year—paring back on stocks and putting more into fixed income bonds as they near retirement. Knowing when to rebalance your portfolio is just as important as knowing what types of investments to carry. A systematic rebalancing of assets can boost returns and lower risk at the same time. For example, let's say that you started a year with a portfolio of 50 percent large-cap stocks, 25 percent international stocks, and 25 percent small-cap stocks. If at the end of the year you find yourself with 60 percent large-cap, 20 percent international, and 20 percent small-cap, you should sell enough of the large-cap, and buy international and small-cap so that you return to the original percentages. Rebalancing should begin, as much as possible, in tax-advantaged accounts such as those of a 401(k) or IRA because there are no tax consequences to moving different funds around.

Rather than selling what you already have to purchase something else, experts recommend that you rebalance the mix by shifting your purchases. If a favorable market has made your portfolio stock-heavy, rebalance by purchasing more bonds. If you sell the stocks to get money to buy bonds for a quick fix, you will end up paying capital gains taxes on the stocks you sold. Most experts urge people to avoid overreacting to market dips. Instead of following the "10 hottest funds" trumpeted in magazine headlines, they advise investors to adopt a more disciplined strategy based on sound theory. And instead of focusing on one particular investment that may be faltering, they suggest looking at the portfolio's overall performance. A word of caution: There are tax consequences to selling stocks that have performed well. Selling losers to offset taxes from winners is the best strategy.

At Bankrate.com, our calculators help you determine how much you should be saving for retirement, college, and emergencies. By answering a few simple questions, you can get a savings plan tailored to your specific situation.

Teaching Tactics Time Line

It's never too early to start teaching kids about money. Plunking pennies into a piggy bank is a good start, but teaching them to save often begins by setting a good example. Seeing you budget each week shows them good savings habits—and that money doesn't grow on trees.

A piggy bank is a great place for three- and four-year-olds to keep their savings. You can help your kids find pictures of the toys or items they want to save for, then tape them to the side of the bank to remind them why they're saving money. And you can teach little ones about money by separating coins into piles by color and size and discuss their value.

Elementary-age kids *can* understand how interest is earned on a savings account, how store coupons work, and how to budget for something they want. They can appreciate how businesses operate and how investors buy and sell stocks. You may want to teach them about stocks by making a game where all family members pick a company and invest $100 phantom or real money and track the stocks' daily progress through the newspaper's financial section.

Preteens can shift a third of their allowances or earnings to satisfy instant, "gotta have it now" urges, a third into short-term savings for a new bike or CD player, and the last third into long-term savings—such as for college.

Many banks let children start savings accounts in their own names with as little as $10. Most will waive penalties for small balances. You might want to match the amount that your child contributes to the account to encourage regular deposits. If you use online banking, you can schedule a weekly or monthly deposit into separate money market accounts for your children. This way, they are less tempted to spend the cash and more likely to learn about interest.

chapter two
BILLS AND CHILLS

Gain Control of Your Expenditures

Do you pay your bills on time? According to Bankrate's 2004 financial literacy survey, more than nine in every ten Americans (95 percent) agree that it's very important to pay bills on time (and thus avoid late fees), yet only 83 percent of them claim that they do so consistently. With interest rates hovering around 12–18 percent for credit cards (1.5 percent on the unpaid monthly balance), the average household pays $1,700 in interest a year, according to Robert D. Manning's *Credit Card Nation*. This is the beginning of a very slippery slope. In fact, eight percent of families have missed a debt payment by two months in a recent year, according to the Federal Reserve. Twenty-three percent have been contacted by a collection agency for a late bill. And as we mentioned in our introduction, 1.65 million declared bankruptcy in 2003.

More than half of those in debt—52 percent of Americans—blame their predicaments on poor money management and ignorance about financial protocols. However, Bankrate's surveys show that people who pay their bills as they come in are more satisfied and less stressed than those who do not. Just the simple habit of paying each bill as it arrives can make a big difference in your quality of life. Here are some more tips for slaying those financial dragons.

- Shift your bills around by changing the due dates on your credit cards. In this way they will not be so heavy during one part of the month. All you have to do is call the customer service number on the bill and speak to a representative.
- If you have a computer and can go online, use your bank's online banking service. Over 35 million Americans use online bill payment today, with that number expected to double in the next five years, according to Jupiter Research. You can schedule a number of your regular monthly payments to take place on the day of your choice. Do not assume that the payment will be executed electronically—assume instead that your bank will send it out by "snail mail." When you schedule your payments, leave time for the check to go through the U.S. postal system. Once you've set up your monthly payments, check your account regularly (two to three times a week) to balance your checkbook and make sure you have enough funds to cover upcoming payments.

   Note: Bankrate studies show that approximately half of banks charge for online banking and bill pay; half do not. The typical charge is between five and eight dollars per month. Search for free online banking services. It engenders a long-term customer relationship between you and your bank. If your bank doesn't offer these services, switch to one that does.
- Always pay your home and auto secured debt promptly—your home and auto are at risk. If you are late on paying unsecured debt, such as your credit cards, your credit rating will suffer and the bank can sue you. But they can't repossess your car or foreclose on your house—like they can if you are unable to keep up with your secured debt payments.

The Bugaboos of Bankruptcy

If you're in way over your head and your finances are ruining your life and your health, it might be worthwhile to consider filing for bankruptcy. (You can only do it once every seven years.)

There are several chapters in the bankruptcy code. Most likely you'll be filing for Chapter 7 protection. This means that your assets will be sold to pay your debts. Which ones will be sold depends on where you live. Most states do not permit creditors to take your home or car, assuming you've got just one. Pretty much everything else, however, is game. The proceeds go into one pot and the creditors are paid according to their priority under the law. Even if the whole debt is not repaid, the slate is wiped clean except for obligations such as student loans, child support, and alimony.

Another bankruptcy option is Chapter 13, but this is only if you have regular income and your unsecured debts (such as credit cards) do not exceed $269,250 and your secured debts (such as a mortgage) do not exceed $871,550. (These numbers are adjusted every three years for inflation.) Most of those who file for Chapter 13 submit a plan to repay all or part of their debts over three to five years. During this time you pay your current bills and turn over your disposable income to a court-appointed trustee, who in turn sends the payments to your creditors. The judge who is hearing the case can switch you to Chapter 7 for liquidation. Attorneys for Chapter 13 often will take their fees through the repayment plan, but those for Chapter 7 filings will probably want their fee ($500 to $1,000) paid up front in cash. A word of caution: If you hide assets, you're committing fraud, a federal offense punishable by a hefty fine and time in prison.

It usually takes three to six months to complete Chapter 7 liquidation. In Chapter 13, the time frame depends on the length of the repayment plan, but it should not be more than five years. Once you file for bankruptcy protection your creditors can no longer try to collect payment and you get to start over with a clean slate. But this will put a permanent black mark on your credit record for ten years; as a result, you'll pay much higher interest rates on credit cards and other credit sources as a high risk. It could also cripple your ability to rent an apartment or to be hired for some jobs. Bankruptcy is an emotional drain as well. It is an absolute of last resort.

In the next chapter, we'll look at surefire ways to keep you out of the debtors' doldrums by sticking to a budget.

chapter three

chapter three
BUDGET BINGO

Create a Comfortable Budget
Recognize Shopping Pitfalls

Do you have a monthly budget? How fastidiously do you follow it? Chances are, unless you're financially buttoned up, you give your "spending plan" mere lip service. Bankrate found proof for this in its 2004 survey, in which 91 percent of Americans said it was important to follow a budget; only 48 percent did so all the time.

The mercurial Mr. Micawber (in Charles Dickens' *David Copperfield*) set the stage for this theme some 150 years ago: "Annual income twenty pounds, annual expenditure nineteen nineteen six, result happiness. Annual income twenty pounds, annual expenditure twenty pounds ought and six, result misery."

Before you get down to the task of drafting a budget, you should determine your net worth—and your current and anticipated financial obligations. This helps determine just how free-spirited or restrained you will need to be when it comes to spending.

Net worth is defined as assets minus all debts. In one column, add up *everything* you own, including money in your savings, checking, retirement accounts, and bonds and equities (from your bank and brokerage statements). Then take a guess on what a buyer would realistically pay for your home, furniture, jewelry, artwork, car, and other items of worth. Now subtract from that *everything* you owe —including credit card, student, and other debt, mortgages, auto loans, monthly expenses for the next six months, and other expenses due. What remains is your net worth (which is *far* different from what you are worth as a person—which, as MasterCard would say, is priceless).

When you recover from the shock of seeing yourself reduced to a number, plow ahead and see how you shape up each month. Jot down in one column how much money comes in each month from salary and other sources of income. In another column note how much is going out each month for housing, food, bills, and miscellaneous expenses.

If you make more than you spend, it's time to plan what to do with the excess. If you spend more than you make, figure out how to trim the fat. Tracking what you spend every day can be tedious—but doable. Track your expenses for a month, keeping a journal of every cent that you spend. Be sure to include quarterly, semiannual, and annual expenses such as your auto insurance that you paid at the start of the year. Divide the expenses evenly so they fit into a monthly budget. In addition, plan for potential emergencies, such as a boiler going on the fritz or an extended bout of pneumonia. Don't forget to figure in savings.

Group your expenses into three categories: *fixed expenses* (mortgage or rent, car payments, insurance premiums, and savings); *variable expenses* (regular bills whose amounts can change, such as electric or phone bills); and *discretionary* (what's left after the basics are covered). If, after comparing the income and outflow of your money you find yourself awash in red ink, it's time to increase your income or decrease your spending. Identify variable costs such as air conditioning and cut back on them. Put your insurance policy out for bids and raise your deductible.

Once you have examined your assets and liabilities, you're ready to draw up a budget (or spending plan) that focuses on where you want your money to go, not on where it shouldn't. Most people would rather visit the dentist than do this, but for most people, making—and sticking to—a budget is the most important step on their way to financial solvency. Even if you have no financial threats on the horizon, the process of drawing up a budget can be eye-opening. You could discover that you are spending more than you thought on gizmos and gadgets and less on things that give you real, lasting pleasure.

Start by listing the sources of income you can rely on month after month. They may include:

- Paychecks
- Social Security
- Pension benefits
- Investment earnings such as bond interest
- Child or spousal support
- Unemployment checks
- If you earn money on an irregular basis, such as tips, or commissions, or income from self-employment, slightly underestimate a monthly average.

Next, examine your checkbook register and credit card statements to determine your core monthly expenses:

- Mortgage or rent payments
- Utilities
- Car payments and other expenses
- Credit card payments

- Groceries and other household staples (an average)
- Child care
- Insurance premiums averaged
- Taxes
- Regular charitable contributions
- Regular savings
- Average of annual expenses for clothing
- Average of annual expenses for medical care
- Average holiday gift buying and special occasions

Then track your voluntary expenses such as:

- Entertainment and dining
- Travel and vacations
- Gifts
- Sports and hobbies

Now compare your monthly expenses to your monthly income. Many people find that while their income exceeds their expenses, they are out of cash by month's end because they've spent far too much on frivolities such as coffee, snacks, and lottery tickets.

It's time now to direct your money before you spend it and control where each dollar goes. Prioritize your expenses and their costs and then negotiate with yourself. Decide which of your expenses you're willing to rein in so that you can move some of the resulting money to higher priorities, such as saving for your retirement, vacation, or your children's schooling.

Here's a look at how average Americans budget their expenses:

○ Housing represents the biggest single expense (comprising any-where from 33 to 37 percent of overall annual expense). Besides turning the thermostat down to save a few bucks or renting out an extra room to generate cash, you can refinance for a better mortgage rate and save hundreds or thousands of dollars every month, depending on the size of your mortgage. In 2004, research from Goldman Sachs showed that 47 percent of mortgages could be profitably refinanced for an average savings of $200 each month. This sum could be the basis of your emergency fund or could help beef up your retirement or college fund savings.

- Food accounts for 15 to 20 percent of the overall expense (so you can set strict limits on discretionary meals, such as a maximum of 5 dollars a week on fast food). Use coupons and look into joining a warehouse food club such as Costco, BJ's, or Sam's Club where you can stock up on certain items in quantity, often at big savings. If you're self-employed, you can deduct from your taxes half of your business-related meals and entertainment and the cost of food for a business party.
- Transportation can take up as much as 13 to 14 percent of your total expenses, so trim back by putting off the purchase of a new car. Experts say that the value of a new car drops by as much as 40 percent in the first two years of ownership. Instead, look into a used car such as a relatively new model that has just come off a one- or two-year lease. It is likely to be in good shape, may have some of its original warranty in place and, best of all, will probably be available at a huge discount off its original price. Don't forget to shop for the best auto insurance rates.
- Clothing accounts for about six to eight percent of total costs annual so consider whether you really need that new sweater or if waiting for a sale will make it look even better.
- Health care represents five to seven percent of the average American's annual expenses, mostly from insurance premiums. So it pays to shop around if you have the option of choosing your insurance carrier. If you work for a large company, make certain you use your employer's flexible spending plan if one is available.

This lets you set aside pre-tax dollars for expenses such as deductibles, copayments and noncovered items such as dentistry and eyeglasses. It does not reduce the cost of health care directly, but it shaves money off the taxes you pay on money that does go toward medical bills. Medical expenses are deductible if they exceed 7.5 percent of your adjusted gross income. Such expenses include not only doctors and hospitals, but also dentists, prescription drugs, medical insurance, and any necessary medical equipment.

○ If you have children, education and child care expenses account for 7 to 11 percent of your overall expenses (not including college). Consider forming a cooperative with other parents where each of you take turns looking after all the children in the group for a certain number of hours a week. If you qualify for the child care credit (a dollar-for-dollar reduction in your taxes), be sure to claim it. To ready junior for college, set up a Coverdell Education Savings Account, formerly known as an Education IRA (which can also be used for pre-college courses). You can also invest with various state prepaid tuition plans where the income is either tax-deferred or completely excluded. Alternatively, or in addition, invest some dollars under your children's names. The income will be taxed to them at their lower rates. Until age 14, the first $750 is taxed to them at a rate of zero, the next $750 is taxed at a ten percent rate, and the excess is taxed at your rate. Once your children hit age 14, up to $26,250 can be taxed to them at 15 percent. Accumulate college savings with these lower-taxed investments.

○ Miscellaneous expenses, 10 to 13 percent of the total, include things such as personal care items, entertainment, and reading materials. You can stock up on personal care items at bulk warehouses, join flat-fee entertainment clubs where you get discounts at restaurants, movie theaters, fast food joints, theme parks, and so on. Check out flea markets and secondhand stores. Instead of pay-ing strangers to mow your lawn or clean your pool, hire your kids.

After you have a budget in place, live with it for a few months until tracking your expenditures becomes almost automatic. Then it's time for you to fine-tune it. Once you have a clear picture of where you are financially and where you want to go, you can adjust your spending and find corners to cut. Do not let your budget become a straight-jacket. You can break the rules every so often. Splurge on occasion like the dieter who grazes without inhibition at a party. But do not just spend money for the sake of spending it. Spend it to enjoy it. Control ling your money means controlling your life. By focusing on your finances instead of avoiding them, you'll make your life easier and hap-pier. You'll be in the driver's seat on the road to financial independence.

Your Spending Self

Find your inner spending demon. Just becoming aware of it can help you control it.

There's a popular saying in ladies' rooms around America: "When the going gets tough, the tough go shopping." For some people, shopping can relieve stress, but using it to avoid problems is akin to a recovering alcoholic taking up the bottle again. It only makes things worse. Some "avoidance" shoppers need to control others and use money to demon-strate their power over another person. (The "breadwinner" splurges to show who is boss.) Others buy for revenge, to punish the mate whose behavior they can't control. Still others try to buy love with money, some-times out of guilt. If you recognize it yourself, the first step is to face the underlying stressor. You may have to resort to professional intervention, such as a credit counselor if the problems primarily involve money, or a marriage counselor or therapist if the problems involve areas other than money. Try to cope with stress in healthier, more positive ways like exercise or sports.

Have you ever returned from a shopping trip to find that you spent more than you planned or bought something you had no intention of buying when you left home? In severe cases, impulse buyers purchase things they do not need and cannot afford, largely because they lack clear financial priorities and want to scratch what itches at that moment. If you tend to buy impulsively, your best defense is to leave the physical presence of the item. Avoid impulsive purchase locations such as malls and department stores and leave the plastic at home. Carry only enough cash to make planned purchases. Market research shows that when shoppers leave the proximity of an item to mull its purchase, they rarely return. Force yourself to compare prices in three locations and use a checklist; this reduces emotional purchases. If the force is greater than you are, put the treasured item on layaway so when calmer thinking returns, you can cancel the purchase if you change your mind. Post a list of desired purchases on your refrigerator door and keep checking it for a few months. This gives you a specific reason to save and helps to reevaluate whether you really want it. Instead of looking at the spending decision as a choice between having something or missing out, see it as a choice between having something trivial now or something bigger you really want later—such as a home or retirement savings.

Shopping Pitfalls

People who have problems with shopping tend to be one of three personality types—the "Fanatical Shopper," the "Passive Buyer" and the "Esteem Buyer."

Fanatical Shoppers drive miles to save a few cents, search for weeks for the lowest price and often buy things they don't need simply because they're on sale. These people define "a penny saved, a dollar wasted." They forget how much their time and energy is worth (even at minimum wage) and beat themselves up over missed savings.

Passive Buyers do not like to shop, so they procrastinate until the eventual purchase costs more, such as delaying brake repairs until the entire brake assembly must be replaced. When they're finally forced to buy, Passive Buyers don't comparison shop so they often pay too much. They often get talked into buying things they don't need or can't afford, allowing the salesperson to decide for them. This is largely because Passive Buyers don't want to be embarrassed by their lack of knowledge about the product; they may want to assign the responsibility to someone else. Passive buying is especially common with investments—where the "shopper" would like to blame someone else when the investment tanks.

Many teens are Esteem Buyers, meaning they *must* have the latest jeans or sneakers to feel like they fit in. Their possessions are badges of success. This is often the youthful version of a commonplace grownup money flaw—keeping up with the Joneses. Esteem Buyers need to recognize that true self-esteem does not depend on material possessions, but from feeling in control of life and having value as a person. The first step is recognizing that the more expensive item is not always the best quality and rarely is the best buy. Devising other ways to feel good, such as taking control of financial decisions, is the second step. Luxuries should be seen as rewards that should be earned. Ask what will really be lost by passing up an item and then make a spending choice later. Decide if an existing or cheaper item can meet the same need and whether this purchase will cause family or financial problems. Come up with a specific purchase you would be willing to drop from your budget for an item that is desired but not needed. This may be enough to make you reconsider.

chapter four
HANGING IT UP

Build Your Retirement Savings

Understand 401(k)s, Defined Benefit Plans, Social Security, IRAs, and Other Pension Plans

Do you contribute to a company-sponsored or Individual Retirement Account (IRA)? According to our Bankrate surveys, 90 percent of Americans believe that they *should* regularly contribute to a company-sponsored retirement account or an IRA, but just over half are actually doing so. This in spite of the fact that 72 percent claim to be good at managing their money!

Most Americans claim they're setting aside money directly from their paychecks to a retirement fund. The problem is, what they're putting into such funds are very modest sums. The median annual contribution to retirement savings is only $3,000. This isn't going to do it. The average pre-retiree will have accumulated just $380,000 by age 62, including home equity, savings, and the future value of pensions and Social Security, according to the National Bureau of Economic Research. This is hardly enough for most people to maintain their standard of living later in life. No wonder 45 percent of workers worry that they'll last longer than their money does!

The median age for retirement today is 63. But two out of five workers expect to retire before turning 62. Whether these elongated retirement years turn out to be blissful or bleak depends a lot on if and how you prepare for them. Furthermore, you can expect government's tendency to increase the retirement age or reduce Social Security benefits to continue, making it more important than ever to look beyond Social Security in planning for your retirement.

Only about a third of Americans take the time to calculate their retirement needs even though doing so is one of the most important things to do in life. The American Savings Education Council says unquestionably that people who calculate their needs are far likelier to hit their target dollar number than those who just plunk an arbitrary amount each year into a 401(k).

The median savings amount retirees anticipated they would need was $400,000 in order to maintain their current lifestyle into retirement, according to Keyport Life Insurance. Even with such modest expectations, 29 percent of people don't expect to have what they need when they retire.

Bankrate suggests that you should count on needing 70 to 90 percent of what you're spending in your pre-retirement life to live a comfortable retirement. (This does not account for inflation.) To figure out the amount of savings you'll need, you could see a financial planner; if you would rather invest in a retirement calculator, there are dozens of personal finance websites (including Bankrate's) offering them for free. Before you sit down to crunch some numbers, remember that the key to a successful retirement is to get started as soon as possible and leave your money untouched so that compounding works for you.

Begin by figuring out how much your present lifestyle costs you. Then think about the type of life you want to lead after retirement.

(Remember to include long-term health care costs.) Map out a financial plan for retiring before 59½ years old and another for retiring after that age. This way you'll know how long you'll be "in harness" and whether it's worth it to take that year's sabbatical to India.

Figure out what assets you have that produce income. You might want to begin investing more aggressively with investments that produce a greater rate of return. Take advantage of tax-deferred opportunities by maximizing the money you put into available retirement funds from your first day of employment.

No matter where you invest, it's best to do so regularly where a fixed amount is deducted automatically from your paycheck monthly and invested in mutual funds. The result is dollar-cost averaging, which means you buy more shares when prices are low and fewer when prices are high.

401(k)s

According to the Profit Sharing/401(k) Council of America, 17.5 percent of all eligible employees did not participate in their 401(k) plans in 1999. Not doing so is tantamount to throwing away money. An employer's matching contribution represents free cash. It provides an immediate and totally risk-free, tax-deferred return on your savings. By not contributing enough to receive the maximum possible match from your employer, you leave money on the table. Not only do you miss out on that money, but you miss out on the compounded growth that money could have earned—a loss that could easily amount to thousands of dollars.

Many 401(k) plans let you borrow money from them. Unless it's a dire emergency, however, it's unwise to take advantage of this. For one thing, you must pay it back. And since you'll lose the interest you would have earned by leaving the money alone, you will reduce the balance that would have been available in the plan at retirement had you not taken the loan.

Many plans today offer a "24/7" ability to switch from one investment to another, allowing the plan participant to chase what's hot. This is called market timing, and it is almost invariably a mistake to do. Even the pros can't divine the market successfully. It is best to be consistent and stick with an appropriate investment allocation of stocks, bonds, and cash—one that you update annually to be sure it reflects your current life situation, age, retirement plans, and risk tolerance.

For example, experts at Bankrate recommend that older workers choose more conservative places to park their retirement funds while younger participants be more aggressive. The rule of thumb is that those with at least ten years until retirement should put most of their investments in equities to ensure the maximum accumulation in their 401(k) accounts—and that they steadily decrease exposure to stocks beginning five to ten years before retirement.

Another common 401(k) mistake is banking most of your retirement money on shares in your own company. At Bankrate we believe you should have no more than 15 to 25 percent of your plan assets in company stock. Or you may find yourself postponing your retirement if the one big egg in your basket cracks.

Many plans today have a default election meaning that unless you specifically opt out of the plan you are automatically reenrolled in it, and your contribution will be made to a default option. Usually this is an ultraconservative choice such as a money market fund. Allowing this automatic election to stand consigns you to low returns. You may actually elect the default option—but make sure it's *your* election.

The majority of Americans cash out their 401(k) balances when they change jobs rather than rolling over the money into another retirement account, according to Hewitt Associates, a management consulting firm. More than 80 percent of employees cash out when balances are $3,500 or less, and more than 30 percent take the money and run even when they have substantial balances of up to $25,000. Spending the amount you have in a retirement plan, rather than reinvesting it, shortchanges you in two ways. First, if you're under age 59½, you'll pay an early-withdrawal penalty plus income tax on the money. Second, in the long term you lose even more because you forfeit the tax-deferred compounding of 401(k) earnings. For instance, with an average eight percent annual interest rate over 30 years, a $5,000 balance would grow to more than $50,000. The greatest flexibility in your investment choices comes with rolling over your balance into an IRA.

Defined Benefit Plans

Traditional pensions, or defined-benefit plans, promise retirees a certain amount of money when they retire based on their years of service and salary as well as the contributions they and their employer have made and the returns earned by the investments. Most company pensions pay out their benefits in the form of an annuity—a fixed monthly payment for the rest of a worker's life. The formula used to calculate the annuity typically includes the final salary, years of service, and a fixed percentage rate (often two percent). When you leave your job, your pension benefits stay in the company-sponsored plan where they can be claimed at age 65. Some pension plans can be tapped even earlier. However, like Social Security, your benefit may be reduced because you will be receiving these payments over a longer period of time.

If you're self employed or a small-business owner you have more choices about when your retirement will be and how to save for it — and this means more responsibility. In addition to Individual Retirement accounts (IRAs), you can create a Simplified Employee Pension Plan (SEP), Keogh, or, if you're running a small business, a Savings Incentive Match Plan for Employees (SIMPLE).

Individual Retirement Account (IRA)

The traditional Individual Retirement Account (IRA pronounced "eye-rah") is an investment account that you open through a bank, brokerage firm, or mutual fund. It allows you to defer taxes on your earnings until you withdraw them. IRAs are called "Individual" Retirement Accounts because you open them in your own name and your name alone. There are no joint IRAs even for married couples. Contributions are tax-deductible in the tax year for which they are made. Under tax legislation passed in 2001, the contribution amounts for individuals younger than 50 will increase incrementally until hitting a $5,000 contribution level in 2008. Older workers also will be able to invest more in their IRAs each year, with the catch-up amount topping out at $1,000 in 2008. You do not have to deposit the same amount of money in your IRA each year. You can also make contributions to more than one IRA. However, each person's total IRA contribution cannot be more than the maximum contribution for that year.

There are three types of IRAs. With the traditional kind, established by Congress in 1974, you do not pay taxes on the money earned here until you start withdrawing the money from it and most people, depending on how much they earn, can deduct their annual

IRA contributions from their taxable income each year. You cannot begin withdrawing money from your IRA until you reach 59½ (if you do, you'll pay a hefty tax penalty) but you must start to take it out when you turn 70½ (if you don't, you'll pay a hefty tax penalty).

With a Roth IRA, which is only available to individuals with certain incomes, you don't pay taxes on the income you earn through your IRA investments as long as your withdrawals comply with IRS rules. This means that your earnings from a Roth IRA grow tax-free over time. But you can't deduct your annual Roth contributions from your taxable income or start using your Roth earnings until you turn 59½. You can keep contributing money to the IRA for as long as you earn money and do not have to withdraw money from the account, or pay additional taxes, when you turn 70½.

The third variety, a Coverdell Education Savings Account, can help you save for the education of a child or grandchild with a maximum contribution of $2,000 a year. Interest, dividends, and capital gains earned from these accounts can be withdrawn tax-free to pay tuition for private and parochial schools from kindergarten through college. You can only contribute to a Coverdell Education Savings Account if you meet IRS income limits.

Simplified Employee Pension Plan (SEP)

A SEP is an employer-sponsored retirement plan for small businesses to cover their owners and employees. It's very much like an IRA but is available to independent contractors, sole proprietors who have no employees and businesses that won't know their financial status until tax time. SEPs can be established *after* the employer's tax year has ended, and contribution amounts can be determined after you see what your profits will be for the year. The most that can be contributed each year is the lesser of 25 percent of compensation up to $205,000 or $41,000 for 2004.

Keogh Plans

A Keogh is a tax-deferred retirement plan for self-employed workers. There are two different types: the profit-sharing type where the contribution amount can change each year and the money purchase type where you must make the same percentage contribution each year, whether you have profits or not. Keoghs have high maximum contributions which can grow tax-deferred until withdrawal (assumed to be retirement), at which time they are taxed as ordinary income. By contributing a good part of your earnings into a Keogh you reduce your taxable salary. You can contribute to a Keogh for a tax year from January 1 of that year until April 15 of the next year.

Savings Incentive Match Plan for Employees (SIMPLE)

A Savings Incentive Match Plan for Employees (SIMPLE) lets employees at businesses with 100 or fewer workers make salary-reduction contributions to an IRA. These SIMPLE plan contributions cannot exceed $6,000 per year, and the contributions must be a percentage of the participant's earnings that is specified by the participant.

Social Security

According to *Are You Normal About Money?* by Bernice Kanner 46 percent of Americans believed in the existence of extraterrestrials while only 28 percent believed Social Security would still be around when they retire!

Social Security benefits are based on what you've contributed to the system over time. They are counted in quarters of years. You need 40 quarters of contributions to be eligible for Social Security benefits. The maximum benefit is around $1,715 per month at retirement. There are survivor benefits attached to Social Security for minor children and surviving spouses. Disability benefits may also be attached, but not everyone qualifies for disability benefits because the definition of disability is very stringent.

You can apply and begin to collect as early as age 62, and as late as age 70. For disability benefits, you should apply within the first year of the disability. For survivor benefits, you should apply as soon as possible after the death of the spouse or parent of minor children.

In 2004, the average retiree collects $804 a month from Social Security. But 70 percent of Americans currently working believe that Social Security won't provide the same amount for them when they're ready to collect, according to the Employee Benefit Research Institute (EBRI). They're right. Many do not even know that they won't be able to collect what they expect at age 65. In fact, 96 percent of current workers will not be eligible for full Social Security benefits when they reach 65, says EBRI, but only 16 percent realize this. In 1983 the Social Security Administration changed the rules to gradually increase the age at which full benefits are paid beginning in 2003 for people born after 1937.

Each year around your birthday, the Social Security Administration sends you a statement estimating the benefits you are due. Notify them of your pending retirement a month or two before it happens. You should arrange for an appointment with a representative of the Social Security Administration in order to fill out the necessary paperwork.

Should you take benefits early or wait instead? Social Security law lets you retire at age 62 with benefits that are permanently reduced.

For those born in 1937 or earlier, this lower benefit is 80 percent of the amount available at the full retirement age of 65. But because you draw benefits longer, you could come out ahead, depending on how long you live. Actuaries feel that whether you take the reduced benefit early or wait until full retirement, you'll get the same amount of money. But as any gambler knows, there are always winners and losers. To help decide how you should bet, request:

- an earnings statement to see a year-by-year breakdown of income
- estimates of retirement benefits before age 65, at full retirement age and at age 70
- the number of earnings credits needed to retire
- the number of credits you have accumulated

Whatever you do, don't collect Social Security early while you're still earning wages. There's a severe penalty involved for doing so.

Four Things to Do to Prepare for Retirement

1. **Shuck off debt.** Consider using savings to wipe away most or all of the debt as soon as possible, provided doing so won't leave you destitute. Once this is done, enjoy yourself while keeping an eye on those balances.
2. **Pay down your mortgage completely before retirement.** You don't get much tax benefit from keeping the loan at this point. You can sell your house for a smaller one (which requires less upkeep) or stay where you are. Either way, you'll reduce living expenses and be mortgage-free. Or you can take out a reverse mortgage, where the bank pays you money every month; the amount you "borrow" is paid back when the house is sold. If

you die while still owning the house, the lender will sell it and your heirs will get the difference between what is owed and the value of the house.

3. Do not count on Social Security to provide for you the way it provided for those who came before you.

4. Do not forget to consider long-term care insurance, Medigap insurance, and life insurance. Long-term care insurance helps to cover what Medicare doesn't, including long-term nursing and rehabilitative and day care services at home, in a community center, or at a nursing home. This is insurance for the middle class. The poor and the wealthy don't need to bother: Medicaid pays for the poor, the wealthy can pay for themselves. Investigate a policy before you turn 50—rates are much lower if you start paying in earlier. Medigap insurance pays for some out-of-pocket medical expenses, such as deductibles and co-insurance and possibly outpatient prescriptions. If your death will not create significant financial hardships for surviving relatives, you probably do not need to buy life insurance.

The Rocky Road

Just 21 percent of us expect that our standard of living in old age will be better than it is now, according to Kanner's book *Are You Normal About Money?* Are you heading down a rocky road? See if you're one of the people described below:

○ One in ten employees whose companies make automatic contributions to a retirement plan for them opt out. The overall participation rate for all 401(k)s is just 67 percent.

○ A third of us have no idea how much we will really need to retire. Having no plan is like driving blindfolded.

○ Some people try to make up for lost time by investing aggressively. Avoid acting on hot stock tips unless it's with money you're ready and willing to lose.

○ 27 percent of folks have tapped their retirement savings to satisfy a whim, to buy a car, fund a vacation, or otherwise snag something big. The cost of tapping your IRA far outweighs the benefit. You would have to pony up the income tax when you file your taxes and pay a 10 percent penalty to boot if you're younger than 59½. You would be trading a small short-term gain today for large long-term benefits when you retire. Early retirement requires discipline, keeping debt down, and perhaps not living it up now.

○ Through no major fault of their own, many people find themselves in a pension pickle. Hundreds of companies have gone bankrupt, leaving those who invested in their 401(k) plans abandoned or, in industry parlance, orphaned. These people cannot get their money. Since 1999, the Labor Department has investigated more than 600 orphaned plans and has protected $220 million in plan assets. The plan assets are protected. They are in a trust, are not subject to creditors, and are under the control of a reputable third-party administrator; the mess, however, takes a long time to unravel.

Read the newspaper and you'll hear daily about corporate pensions that are seriously underfunded. Indeed, a report by Merrill Lynch says that most of the 348 S&P 500 companies with defined-benefit plans have liabilities that exceed their assets. This means that if you're asleep at the switch not monitoring your plan, you could be in for a rude awakening. Ask your company's plan administrator for documents such as the Summary Plan Description, Summary of Material Modifications, and Individual Benefit Statements. If he or she is uncooperative, report them to the Department of Labor. Keep track of your 401(k) if you leave it with your old company. Do not make the mistake of abandoning your own plan and then trying to track it down years later when you want to start taking distributions. Most experts recommend rolling over your 401(k) from the company you're leaving into an IRA.

Most defined-benefit plans are insured by the Pension Benefit Guaranty Corporation (PBGC), a government corporation charged with making sure employees of a company that goes bankrupt or can no longer support the pension plan get at least minimum benefits. But the guarantee of the pension is only as good as the guarantee of your firm and the PBGC. If the firm is in jeopardy, compare your monthly benefit with what the PBGC plan currently guarantees. If there is a big enough gap, and in many cases there are, people who retire end up with a lower pension than they thought; they must then fill that gap. The maximum benefit that PBGC would currently pay someone who retires at age 65 is $43,977. A 60-year old retiree would get at most $28,500 and a 70-year old retiree, $73,000. If your plan allows a lump sum withdrawal and you sense the firm is in trouble or about to merge or be acquired, take advantage of this option.

There are ten reasons to contact the U.S. Department of Labor. Do so if:

1. Your statement is consistently late or comes irregularly. You should get an Individual Benefit Statement at least once a year if the employer is the only contributor and quarterly if you are also contributing.
2. The account balance does not look as if your employer's contribution was credited to you.

3. Your employer did not send your contribution to the plan in a timely manner, suggesting he or she used your retirement plan contributions as "float."
4. Your balance has dropped significantly and cannot be explained by market ups and downs.
5. Your statement shows that the contribution from your paycheck was never made.
6. Investments listed on your statement are not the ones you authorized.
7. Former employees are having trouble getting their benefits paid on time or in the correct amounts.
8. There are unusual transactions listed, such as a loan to your employer, a corporate officer, or one of the plan trustees in the Summary Annual Report, which you should get automatically every year from your plan administrator.
9. There are frequent and unexplained changes in investment managers or consultants.
10. Your employer has experienced severe financial difficulty.

Other than your IRA and pension plan and salary, there are ways to save for retirement and live the good life by taking advantage of other job perks. Sadly, most workers do not know where all the sweets are.

Three out of four people who have life insurance as part of their compensation packages do not even know they have it (and many buy their own additional insurance outside the company). Two out of three do not know they're covered by a policy that would pay them a regular wage until their normal retirement age in cases of illness and injury, and 15 percent do not know that they're covered by a corporate pension plan.

While salary is the top financial benefit job seekers weigh, it's certainly not the only one. Other key considerations are bonuses and incentives, time off, reimbursement for relocation costs, and the frequency and assurance of performance reviews with an option for raises and promotions.

Other Sugar in the Salt Mine

IRAs and company pension plans are not the only perks available. Do you know all that your company is offering so that you can take advantage of it?

What Is Your Company Offering?

- 62 percent of companies offer paid time off plans; the figure was 33 percent five years ago.
- 28 percent offer flexible spending accounts (which allow employees to set aside pre-tax dollars for dependent care, medical care, and health care premiums); this is up from 20 percent in 1997.
- 43 percent of companies offer retirement planning services; this figure was 33 percent five years ago.
- 25 percent of companies offer domestic partner benefits for same-sex partners and 16 percent offer benefits for opposite-sex partners; this figure compares with 6 percent reporting domestic partner benefits in 1997.
- 58 percent of companies offer cash-out sick leave upon retirement, this is up from 33 percent five years ago.
- 45 percent offer cash/pay for unused sick leave and one in three offers sick leave sharing/leave banks.
- 11 percent convert sick leave to vacation time.

- 9 convert sick leave to insurance at retirement.
- 3 percent convert sick leave to disability insurance.
- 2 percent convert sick leave to wellness expenses.
- While more than one in three job offers made to executives include a guaranteed severance package equal to 8.12 months of pay on average, lower level workers do not play in this league. Similarly, 40 percent of companies offer signing bonuses to top-level managers, 45 percent offer stock options to them, and 72 percent now offer performance bonuses. Forty-one percent offer performance reviews within the first six months on the job and 34 percent offer guaranteed first year bonuses.

What Our Retirement Funds Look Like

- Four out of five families have at least one 401(k) retirement plan. The average account balance is near $40,000, according to the 2000 Federal Reserve survey. Just ten percent of Americans have more than $100,000 in one of these plans.
- 22 percent have both a pension and a 401(k) plan.
- Although a Roth IRA offers a tremendous tax break for people who can put away $3,000 a year and let it grow, only seven percent of Americans have one.
- 55 percent of workers expect the bulk of their retirement income to come from Keoghs, IRAs, and 401(k) plans, while 44 percent are counting most heavily on their personal mutual funds, stocks and bonds, savings, and annuities. The rest foresee inheriting money or getting their children to help them financially. Twenty-two percent envision having income from another job post-retirement. Fifty-five percent expect their employers will also provide post-retirement health care coverage. This may not be a safe bet—as fewer employers are now providing them.

chapter five
BANK ON IT

Check Up on Your Bank
Know What Records to Keep and Where to Keep Them

Do you read your bank account statements regularly? While Bankrate's surveys found that 74 percent of Americans do it all the time, more than half do not reconcile their bank statements regularly, if ever. Many people do not even open the envelope with their bank statement inside. Don't be one of them. Banks frequently make mistakes. It's your job to catch them.

From what we see at Bankrate, perhaps the biggest problem is that Americans do not think they can negotiate with their banks. Nonsense! You have a good chance of negotiating no-fee checking, no-fee credit cards, lower credit card interest rates, and a discount on your safe deposit box. Consumer banking has become very competitive in the United States, and the worst thing that can happen for a bank is to lose a good retail customer—it's anathema to them. Your lifetime value as a customer is significant, and if you threaten to switch banks, often you can get what you want. Get to know your branch manager and start asking for breaks. Plus, your life will be much easier when something goes awry.

Other than not checking bank statements, many Americans make other costly banking boo-boos. Here are some you should avoid:

- Don't keep more than $100,000 at any one bank. The Federal Deposit Insurance Corporation limits protection to $100,000 per person (not per account as many people believe) at each financial institution where you deal.
- Don't order checks from your bank. You can get them elsewhere for less. (It's not necessary to include your address on the check and many experts recommend omitting it as a safety measure to avoid identity theft.)
- Make sure you have enough money in your bank account before you write a check. It's embarrassing, time-consuming, and costly to bounce a check. Bankrate's research shows the national average fee for a bounced check came to $25.80 in 2003, with fees going as high as $35! If you have bounced several checks in the past year, look at some form of overdraft protection from your bank.
- Think twice before locking into a five-year CD at a low rate, without "laddering" into shorter-term CDs as well. Bankrate.com publishes a CD Rate Trend Index each week summarizing where investment professionals think interest rates are heading and showing where the highest CD rates are offered.
- Try to avoid withdrawing money from a bank where you do not have an account. Sure, it's convenient—but the convenience comes with a price. Bankrate studies show non-bank ATM withdrawals cost an average of $2.69 between the surcharge by ATM owner and the fee charged by your bank. So for a $50 withdrawal, the almost three dollars in fees represents a six percent transaction cost. This for taking money out of your own account!
- Don't pay a bank for its services. Rather, let them pay you. Add enough to your minimum account balance so that it becomes fee-free.

o Make sure your CD is not callable, meaning it can be redeemed anytime the issuer wants. It will not be called if interest rates go up but if the rates drop, the issuer will probably redeem it, leaving you to reinvest when everything else is similarly in the dumps. It's a heads-I-win/tails-you-lose situation—for the bank.

o Don't succumb to the lure of "early withdrawal." Federal law requires a minimum penalty of seven days interest for early withdrawal on any account classified as a time deposit. Since the law does not set a maximum penalty, banks are free to (and usually do) charge much more. Before opening a CD account, find out all the details.

o Don't put all your eggs in one basket. Unless you're extraordinarily lucky you'll be taken for a bumpy ride. Rather, allocate your assets. This means divvying up the eggs in your basket so that you spread the risk.

It's also your job to know where your important papers are and, if you had five minutes to clear out of your house, what you should grab. Here are some tips to help you plan for the unthinkable:

• Identify a single location to file all crucial papers—a fireproof box or safe deposit box.

• Create copies now (certified, in cases of birth certificates and other crucial documents) in case you need to provide them to government agencies.

• Put important original documents in plastic covers to protect them and to prevent you from accidentally giving away the original.

• Tell friends or relatives where important information is located in case you're not available when it is needed.

• Identify the records that you or your financial institutions keep only on computer. They may not be available if electrical power fails, so make printouts.

- Keep your marriage records, divorce decrees, and birth certificates in a safe deposit box. Keep a record of bank accounts, identification records (driver license, green card, passport, and so on), titles, deeds, registrations for property and vehicles owned, mortgages, and other loan information.

Here are some other things to safeguard:

- Insurance policies
- Investment records
- Credit card statements
- Employer benefit statements
- Income tax information (copies of past returns, proof of estimated tax payments)
- Report of earnings from Social Security
- Social Security card
- Trusts
- Wills

Other precautionary steps:

- It's a good idea to keep one key to the safe deposit box in the house and one with another person (a relative or lawyer).
- Itemize objects room by room, filling in serial numbers, purchase dates and estimated values.
- Keep backups away from your home and update your computer files regularly, adding these records to your safe deposit box.
- Keep a notebook with contact information for banks and other financial institutions, your employer, insurance agents, and utility companies.

chapter six
WILLING IT

Decide Who Gets What
How to Give It to Them
A Look at the Deadly Business of Funerals

Have *you* prepared a will? By and large, Americans are too busy living to think about dying. Despite the fact that nearly nine out of ten Americans consider it important to prepare a will, only 42 percent of Americans have one, Bankrate surveys had found. Wills are the area where there is the greatest gap between knowing and doing—and, depending on the size of your estate, it is a gap that is very easy to close. It does not have to cost a lot—according to Kanner's book *Are You Normal About Money?*, 21 percent of people with a will prepared it without a lawyer, with the help of a do-it-yourself manual.

Seven out of ten Americans die *intestate*, meaning they have no will stating what they want to have happen after they die. (This means, of course, that the courts decide, based on state law, who smiles.) Amazingly, four in ten of those who have not prepared a will do not plan to do so before they die.

Everyone who is of legal age (usually 18) and mentally competent should have a will, even if the person doesn't have a king's ransom to leave behind. In fact, despite all the talk about the burgeoning number of millionaires in this country, 93 percent of Americans have estates that add up to less than $1 million. A fourth of those who make wills doubt that they will have anything of real value to leave. But they should definitely still make one. Wills are about more than what happens to your money and possessions. They're about whom you (the testator if you are a man or testatrix if you are a woman) want to finish raising your minor children and who will be in charge of making sure your wishes are carried out (an executor or executrix). Parents often dawdle here because they think that no one will be the perfect guardian. But a pretty good one whom you select is still a whole lot better than leaving your child's destiny in the hands of the state.

Wills can be changed as often as your life circumstances or desires do. But be sure that your latest document notes the date and proclaims that this is your last will and testament, prepared by you while you were of sound mind and body and supersedes all prior wills you have made.

Ideally, your will should:

○ Name a guardian for your children and for their money and possessions.
○ Name an executor to make sure your wishes as stated in the will are carried out.
○ Stipulate where the money to pay taxes, debts, and your funeral should come from.
○ Be signed by two witnesses who are not beneficiaries in the will. (By signing the will, they could lose what you wanted them to inherit.)
○ Not contain dollar amounts but percentages instead

o Not contain special burial instructions such as a desire to be cre-
mated

You do *not* need to get overly specific about distribution of personal effects. First of all, you can distribute cash or possessions worth
up to $11,000 per year ($22,000 per couple) without incurring a gift
tax. This will lessen the taxable value of your estate. Second, you
may want to leave a few items to specific relatives and friends in a
separate letter to your executor. It's not necessary to include it in the
will. Third, Bankrate recommends that your personal effects be
appraised upon your death, and a list of items be prepared with the
indications of value. Then surviving relatives participate in a "round
robin." In this process, each beneficiary you want included in the
process takes turns choosing what items they want, with the oldest
child going first (for example), or drawing straws to establish the
order of participation. At the end of the process, the remaining items
are sold or donated, the value of each beneficiary's choices is established, and then cash distributions are made to even things out.

To prepare a will you can hire an attorney you trust or you can do
it yourself with the help of will-writing programs or books. An
excellent program is Nolo Press's "Willmaker Plus," available at
www.nolo.com. An attorney will usually do a bare-bones or simple
will (meaning no trusts and an estate value under $1 million) for less
than $100.

If you have at least $250,000 to leave, you might want to set up a
living trust, an agreement between you, the *grantor* who establishes
and funds the trust, and the *trustee*, who administers it. When someone with a living trust dies, he or she can leave all his assets to the
trust, which can then be doled out by the trustee. This escapes the
attorney's fees (usually about two to three percent of the estate) for

presenting the will to the court. Living trusts also get the assets into the heirs' hands more quickly (60 to 90 days rather than nine months or so for probate). An attorney will set up a living trust for $500 to $1,000, and there is a yearly maintenance fee charged by the institution that houses it.

Living Wills

Most individuals have their living wills and durable powers of attorney prepared at the same time they prepare their last will and testament. But don't wait too long. Anything can happen at any time and you want to be in control of your health care decisions even if you become incapacitated. A living will makes your health care wishes known ahead of time. Appointing a durable power of attorney for health care assures that they'll be followed.

A living will is a legal document in which you direct your physician to withdraw life support if you become terminally ill, or find yourself in an irreversible coma or vegetative state and are no longer capable of making your own decisions. Your living will should address what your physician is to do about resuscitation, life support, a ventilator, antibiotics, a feeding tube, intravenous artificial hydration, pain medication and oxygen therapy, and "do not resuscitate" orders. You can make your living will very specific.

Although a living will directs your doctor how to handle the situation when you are terminal, it's a good idea to have a durable power of attorney for health care, an agent or proxy you appoint to make medical decisions based on your previously stated wishes, and a backup should the appointed person choose not to make what could be a very difficult decision. The health care agent appointed through a durable power of attorney can make other types of health care and treatment decisions for you if you are not competent to do so yourself. Be sure to give your physician and health care agent copies of the documents. You can change the terms of your living will and durable power of attorney for health care at any time.

Funerals

A funeral service is right up there with buying a car for expense (but, we'd wager, not enjoyment). During what is usually a highly emotional time, shoppers are often pressured or guilt-tripped into buying pricey funeral goods or services that they do not need or want. According to the American Association of Retired Persons, funeral and burial costs can easily reach $10,000. The average cost of a traditional adult funeral in 1999 was $5,020 without any extras. Burial costs can add an extra $2,000 or more. Flowers, obituary notices, burial liners or vaults, limousines, and acknowledgement cards—can all add up to a major expenditure.

To prevent yourself from being pressured into buying funeral paraphernalia that you do not want (and then end up having to spend years paying it off), you should shop around. Prices vary tremendously. Experts recommend getting quotes from at least three sources, yet just 54 percent of Americans expect to bury loved ones with any benefit of comparison shopping.

The law requires funeral homes to give you a written price list for goods and services. Ask for it to help keep your emotional trigger under control. Prices should include the initial conference, consultations, paperwork and overhead, or a "nondeclinable fee" added to the total cost of the funeral. There is wide variation in pricing the nondeclinable fee. The general price list should also include cost of transportation of the body, care of the body (including embalming), and use of the funeral home for the viewing, the wake, visitation, and the funeral or memorial ceremony. Alternative arrangements such as cremation and optional services such as flowers, placing an obituary, and obtaining a death certificate should also be listed on the general price list. Embalming is rarely required when the person is to be buried within 24 to 48 hours, although some unscrupulous morticians push it and pretend that it is required. Refrigeration is a less costly option. If a funeral director refuses to allow a public viewing without embalming, you can ask for a private viewing without embalming. The process is very invasive for a temporary cosmetic effect.

Sealed caskets cost hundreds of dollars more than unsealed caskets, but do not protect or preserve the body any better than unsealed. The casket is the single costliest item in a traditional funeral—with an average price approaching $2,000. While caskets were once sold only by funeral homes, today you can buy one on the Internet or use a family-built one if you choose. A funeral home cannot charge a handling fee if you wish to bring in your own casket from an outside source (they're often available for much less). Know that you do not have to buy a package of services the funeral home is pushing: You can and should choose à la carte. You can also have a memorial service at home, your church, a park, or the community center for much less money than at a funeral home. You can cut costs by limiting the viewing to a day or an hour before the funeral and by dressing your loved one in a favorite outfit instead of costly burial clothing.

The Funeral Consumers Alliance has 115 chapters in 46 states around the country. Staffed by volunteers, they have information on local funeral homes as well as price surveys that can help you comparison shop for services. Some have even negotiated discounts with local funeral homes.

chapter seven
GOT INSURANCE?

Disability Insurance: The Gory Details

Life Insurance: How Much Do You Need?

Other Insurance You Need—or Not

How regularly do you shop around for the best insurance quotes and coverage? Chances are, not often enough. According to Bankrate's surveys, 89 percent of Americans say that it is important to shop around for the best insurance quotes and coverage, but just 33 percent actually do it consistently. Three out of five admit they don't know how much life, auto, and health insurance they should carry.

Insurance is there to protect against the unlikely and the unthinkable. Whether it's automotive, health, life or homeowners coverage, insurance may well be the only product that you hope to never use. But not comparison shopping may mean paying far more than you need to.

When you buy insurance you're paying a company for the promise to compensate you if a specified undesired event occurs. Years ago, most people purchased insurance at the kitchen table. Now, an increasing number use the Internet to shop for free quotes.

Health Insurance

Some 44 million Americans—one in seven—have no health insurance. For those who do, nearly 85 percent receive it through their employer or their spouse's employer. While companies still pay the bulk of their workers' health care costs, their contributions have slipped in recent years and now hover around 70 percent. This means that workers' copayments and deductibles are up. Even though the stakes are high here, just 17 percent of us spend more than an hour reading our health-plan manuals. Fewer than half read the materials with anything more than a cursory glance—until we need to make a claim.

The Three C's to Consider

1. Coverage. Take into account your personal needs for health care coverage. Do you have any special medical needs? Insurance plans can include maternity coverage, prescription costs, annual physicals, dependent coverage, specialists' coverage, and more. The more benefits you select, the greater your premium will be. (A premium is the amount you pay monthly.)
2. Convenience. Health maintenance organizations (HMOs) limit your choice of doctors or hospitals. You have to use a physician included in their plan or fork over extra money to see a doctor who is not included. Be sure you understand how your insurance company defines an emergency and what special steps, if any, you need to take before coverage kicks in. With many plans you are required to get a referral from your primary care physician before seeing a specialist. This could be very inconvenient.
3. Cost. Whether as an individual or part of a company plan, you will still be laying out some of your cash for your medical care. Your premium will depend on what type of plan you choose,

the extent of benefit coverage, and the amount you accept for deductible, coinsurance and copayment.

Think about the state of your health and lifestyle, and consequently the likely frequency that you'll seek medical care. If you are healthy and expect to stay that way, consider adopting a higher copay and a lower premium. If you're the sort who considers a 99-degree temperature good reason to take to your bed, you may be better off paying a higher premium and paying less for each doctor's visit.

Many companies now offer flex dollars, allocating a certain amount to all medical or health services from dentistry to corrective lenses and bone density tests. Most consumer-driven plans combine a high deductible (at least $1,000) with an employee reimbursement account from which medical bills are paid. The specific account type—health reimbursement arrangement, medical savings account, or medical expense reimbursement plan—depends upon company size and how coverage is structured. It's a little like a flexible spending account (FSA) except that this last one is an add-on to your company's health care program.

Your account is funded either by your employer, by regular contributions that come out of your paycheck, or both. Again, the amounts and payment frequency depend on your plan specifics. If set up carefully, the account should be more than enough to pay for an annual physical and a couple of visits to the doctor for minor complaints. But if you have a serious illness, unexpected medical problems or a chronic condition that requires expensive treatment, you'll quickly exhaust your reimbursement stash. Then you must to come up with the deductible amount.

The good news is that once you have exhausted your medical account and have met your coverage's deductible, the plans usually pay 100 percent of care costs. But for many workers, the combined reimbursement account and deductible costs can be very painful, especially if you have to come up with it every year.

Insurers and employers like these accounts because they make workers consider the high cost of health care. Despite the potential for big medical payments, some employees also like them because they often offer more freedom than managed care in deciding which caregiver to use. Under certain circumstances, the reimbursement account is a tax-free benefit. And many companies allow employees to either pocket any excess or roll it over into next year's account.

If you're young enough or in college, you can probably still be covered by your parents' insurance. If you're working, you may be able to get health insurance from your employer, which is about the cheapest way to get it. If you're between jobs and your prior company offered medical benefits, you can extend your coverage via COBRA, a 1985 federal law called the Consolidated Omnibus Budget Reconciliation Act. It requires employers to allow former employees and their dependents to pay for continued insurance coverage for up to 36 months after they leave their jobs.

If you are working at a small company with few benefits or are underemployed, you can look to qualify for a group discount at alumni, professional, religious, or interest groups. Or if you buy an individual policy, consider a temporary three-month plan if you are anticipating starting a new job or enrolling in college, and try to get a discount on your health insurance.

Long-Term or Disability Insurance

Accidents happen. And while there may be little you can do to avoid them, subscribing to long-term disability insurance (or DI in industry speak) can protect your ability to earn an income. Statistically, your chance of being disabled at age 40 is much higher than your chance of dying. The Department of Housing and Urban Development notes that half of all mortgage foreclosures are the result of a disabling injury or illness. Yet, three out of five working adults in America do not have disability insurance, according to the Health Insurance Association of America.

Before you rush out to buy any, however, find out from your company benefits manager whether you already have long-term benefits and if so, what they cover. Interestingly, most policies exclude coverage under military service or from war or terrorism. Most DI plans pay you 60 percent of your income—enough to cover the basics, but not enough to make disability worry-free. Because employer plans only cover 60 percent of your compensation, it can be a big oversight to ignore buying supplemental disability insurance in addition to the coverage you receive through your employer, especially if you are the sole support of your family. If you have covered your other insurance basics—medical, life, homeowners, and auto—and you are the sole supporter of your family, Bankrate strongly recommends that you fill out your disability coverage with a supplemental policy.

Few policies pay for life. These policies, after all, are designed to substitute for income during your working years and the assumption is that you'll retire someday and receive retirement benefits. The premium will depend on an array of factors such as your age, your sex (women pay more as they tend to live longer, sicklier lives than men), how risky your job is, your income, medical history, and lifestyle, including whether you smoke.

If you have "own occupation" coverage, you are assumed to be disabled when you cannot perform the functions of *your* job. With "any occupation" coverage, your coverage will not be triggered until a doctor declares you're unable to work at *any* job for which you have been reasonably trained. Get a policy that specifies "own occupation" coverage. The *elimination period* determines when after 30 days you start receiving benefits. Whether this elimination period is 60, 90, or

120 days can lower the premium. If you have a claim, file it as soon as possible because that starts the clock for the elimination period.

Life Insurance

Though death is a certainty, you probably do not need life insurance, unless you have school-age children, a nonworking spouse, or parents who are unable to take care of themselves. Many employers include a basic death benefit in their insurance package that is usually just enough to cover burial expenses and pay a few bills. This is fine if you are single, but you definitely need more coverage if your responsibilities include dependents.

The most basic type, term insurance, pays your beneficiary only if you die during a specific term while you're paying a fixed premium annually. Term insurance is flexible in that you can pay for the insurance while your children are dependent on you, and then drop the coverage when they are out of the nest. If you are not rich, term insurance tends to be the best deal because you get the most coverage for the least amount of premium.

Wealthier people often opt for permanent life insurance—whole life, universal life or variable life. Whole life is like term insurance in that you have set premiums for a set benefit, but the policy has no ending date. You pay the premium for the rest of your life unless you cash in and receive the value as a lump sum. The cash value is different from the face amount. With universal life, the insurer separates the death benefit from the investment portion of the premiums. The investments pay for the death benefit. No matter how well or poorly your investments do, you are guaranteed a minimum death benefit. With variable life, the amount of the death benefit varies depending on how well the investment portion of the policy does.

For most Americans, term insurance makes the most sense during child-rearing years. Bankrate.com lists insurance brokers who can help you find the program that is best and most cost-efficient for you. Check your insurance company's Claims Paying Rating, available from A.M. Best. This rating reflects the record for paying claims of the insurer covering your claim. Companies such as Metropolitan Life and Northwestern Mutual have the highest claims paying ratings, but their policies are more expensive.

How much life insurance should you buy? Bankrate recommends at least three to five times your annual salary and bonus. This level of death benefit allows your family enough breathing room to adjust their finances to compensate for the loss of your income from the family budget. A higher level of five to seven times annual compensation can help fund college and retirement needs to which you would have contributed.

Three out of four of us—76 percent—have life insurance, the most popular variety being term insurance, followed by whole life. Just 11 percent have universal life coverage, but this is more than the eight percent who have variable life coverage. A third have at least one policy with cash value built in while 24 percent do not have any.

Homeowners Insurance

Some 88 percent of homeowners and 23 percent of renters have home insurance but only six percent of homeowners have a government-subsidized insurance policy such as flood insurance. What you pay for your homeowners insurance can vary by hundreds of dollars depending on a number of factors, including the company from which you buy your policy, where you live, and how high you've set your deductible. Nowadays, most insurance companies recommend a deductible of at least $500. If you can afford to raise that to $1,000, you may save as much as 25 percent of the premium.

If you live in a disaster-prone area, your insurance policy may have a separate deductible for certain kinds of damage, such as that caused by windstorms, hailstorms, or earthquakes. But there are things you can do to make your home more resistant to windstorms and other natural disasters: Add storm shutters, reinforce your roof, or buy stronger roofing materials. Older homes can be retrofitted to make them better able to withstand earthquakes. In addition, consider modernizing your heating, plumbing, and electrical systems to reduce the risk of fire and water damage. You can usually get discounts of at least five percent off your insurance for a smoke detector, burglar alarm, or dead-bolt locks. Some companies offer to cut your premiums by as much as 15 or 20 percent if you install a sophisticated sprinkler system and a fire and burglar alarm that rings at police, fire, or other monitoring stations. You can also explore getting a group insurance homeowners policy through professional, alumni, and business groups.

If you have kept your coverage with a company for several years, you may receive a special discount for being a long-term policyholder. Some insurers will reduce their premiums by five percent if you stay with them for three to five years and by ten percent if you remain a policyholder for six years or more. But make certain to periodically compare their price with that of other companies' policies to be sure it really is a good deal. Review the limits in your policy and the value of your possessions at least once a year.

Insuring Tiger and Rover

A joint survey from the American Veterinary Medical Association, American Animal Hospital Association, and Association of American Veterinary Medical Colleges found that dogs run up the highest bills of all pets. Their owners paid an average of $1,042 to keep their favorite pet from dying, as opposed to the $657 limit cat owners put on the same scenario.

Pet insurance policies resemble a cross between indemnity products and automobile coverage, with many options in between. Expect to pay a deductible, a copay, or both. Some companies reimburse on a benefit schedule, others opt for a flat payback that typically covers 80 percent of medical expenses. Most plans impose annual payout limits between $10,000 and $12,000; you can raise that by buying a deluxe package policy. Levels of care range from an accident-only policy to comprehensive coverage with a maintenance rider that pays for checkups and teeth cleaning. Most plans in the middle pay for gastrointestinal upset, dermatitis, ear infections, bladder infections, asthma, skin tumors, cancer, diabetes, broken bones, X-rays, diagnostic tests, surgery, anesthesia, hospitalization, prescriptions, and lab fees.

According to a recent American Animal Hospital Association survey, 1 percent of pet owners carry this insurance, with the average premium around $141 each year. But these numbers are growing. Make sure you read the fine print to determine how much bang you'll get for your buck. Never buy a policy from a company not licensed in your state. Without this protection, the company could go under and leave you holding the bag for outstanding treatments and unused premiums.

Insurance You Probably Don't Need

The list of policies that fit this description is an ever-changing one, as insurance companies—like all other businesses—continually develop new products for their customers. How can you tell if a policy is worth it?

One thing to watch for is a policy that is unreasonably complicated. That is especially true with insurance contracts, which can contain numerous clauses and provisions that exclude any number of possible occurrences.

Another red flag is coverage that is very narrowly defined. Policies promising to cover you against cancer are a case in point. Without a doubt, you'll want this protection. However, most—if not all—major medical insurance policies cover cancer, just as they cover other diseases. It is typically less expensive to obtain comprehensive, broad-based coverage, rather than purchase several policies that each focus on a specific disease or condition.

You probably do not need the following:

o An extended warranty to cover repair if the appliance breaks after the manufacturer's warranty has expired. Most defects you'll notice within the first few months when they are still covered by the manufacturer's warranty. And it can cost just as much to replace the broken appliance as it is to pay for the extended warranty.

o Rental car insurance to cover you in case you get in an accident while driving a rental car. If you have standard levels of home-owners, renters, auto, and life insurance, you're already protected for a large number of travel-related incidents in the United States. Most auto policies cover accidents you have in a rental car or offer this coverage through a rider at much cheaper rates.

o Life insurance sold by credit card and mortgage companies to pay any balance remaining on your account when you die. This is what life insurance is for, and it is typically cheaper to obtain coverage through a term life insurance policy than through policies offered by credit card companies. Experts say that as a rule, it doesn't make sense to buy specialty coverage.

o Crime insurance to cover against the expense of being a crime victim such as home invasion, stalking, carjacking and child abduction. The company will pay relevant medical and psychiatric bills

and reimburse lost wages, among other expenses. The policies, which are available in about eight states, run about $100 annually.
o Unreasonably low deductibles. Boosting your deductible by even a modest amount can mean significant savings.

Sometimes, buying your homeowners, auto, and liability coverage from the same company will result in a savings of five to fifteen percent off your premium.

chapter eight
DRIVING MR. WASHINGTON

Lease or Buy?
Showroom Errors
Insure Your Wheels

There's a saying on the car lot; it says that to get the best deal, you should wait until the last month of the model year or from July to October as dealers clear out last year's models at low prices to clear space for new models. But with cash rebates and low-interest financing now *de rigueur*, you may be able to score in any season. To negotiate best, you'll want to know the dealer's cost and incentives, how the dealer makes money and what the car will cost from comparable merchants. Yet, amazingly, just two out of three of us—64 percent—comparison shop for a new car or research its sticker price.

The Internet is making the car buying process more efficient. Bankrate's Annual Car Buying Guide, reports you can order from Consumer Reports and Edmunds.com, and online car buying services such as Autobytel.com and Cars.com make it much easier for you to negotiate for a better price for the car that you want.

Deep down, despite our avowed distaste for haggling for a car, most buyers seem to like it. According to the Dohring Company, almost seven of ten folks who bought a car recently (67 percent) actually enjoyed their last negotiation process. Why? They came prepared and aware.

Often the seller will try to play little games. Sometimes manufacturers up the prices to compensate for incentives or charge extra for features that were once standard. Or the dealer can swindle you negotiating the price of a trade-in, and then again in the business office after negotiations are over. Sometimes dealers secretly hike the price, writing a contract for more than you agreed to. Sometimes they "accidentally" leave your trade-in off the contract, "forget about" the rebate, or add another fee. They occasionally charge the normal lease rate for those who opt for a single upfront payment at a lesser lease rate. Some unscrupulous dealers even charge for options that are not visible, such as a sport suspension or a higher-end stereo system. Most leasing companies charge an acquisition fee or lease origination fee (usually around $450) to open a lease. Your best negotiating ammunition is knowledge—and your best protection is reading the contract carefully before you sign.

To Lease, Perchance to Buy

A lease is essentially a rental agreement whereby you pay monthly installments covering interest and depreciation of the value of the car. In 1990, just ten percent of cars that drove off the lot were leased. A decade later, one in three were.

There are advantages to leasing: low down payments (you can often negotiate a better deal than initially offered), low monthly payments (as you're only paying off the car's depreciation and not its full value) and easy turnover (no trade-in or selling headaches for you). And there are tax benefits. When you buy a car, you pay sales tax on the entire value of the car. When you lease, you pay a use tax on just the amount of value that you will use up during the lease.

There are also disadvantages to leasing: You build no equity (your payments do not go towards owning anything), have little flexibility (bailing out early could cost you as much as six extra months of payments), and face high fees for each mile you drive over a certain limit (typically 12,000 to 15,000 a year) and for excess wear and tear. Leasing a car can bring on higher insurance rates since you may require more coverage than you're used to paying. And you need excellent credit to be accepted as a lessor. Bankrate has an excellent calculator to help you decide whether leasing or buying your next car is the right choice: www.bankrate.com/carlease.

Leasing makes sense if:

○ you need cash.
○ you want new wheels every three years or so.
○ you drive fewer than 15,000 miles a year and maintain a car in good condition.
○ you are able to deduct part of your car's depreciation from your taxes. Interest paid on loans to purchase a car is not deductible but depreciation as well as the implicit financing costs are.
○ you are easy on a car.
○ you have a clear idea where you will be in two or three years (and don't expect to bail early).
○ you trust the company with which you're entering a complex financial relationship.

Purchasing makes sense if:

○ you have cash and reserves.
○ you want new wheels every seven or eight years.

- you drive more than 15,000 miles a year.
- you value the flexibility of being able to bail out of a relationship.

Whopper Wheely Mistakes

Following are several things to avoid when you are leasing or buying a car.

- Getting an open-end lease. In a closed-end lease, you may return the car at the end of the lease and walk away, responsible only for certain end-of-lease charges, such as excess mileage, wear and tear, and disposition. An open-end lease charges the victim the difference between the market value of the car and its predetermined residual value. Open-end leases are very rare in the market today.
- Being so captivated by the shiny new coupe you just bought that you didn't pay enough attention to the financing deal—and were later shocked at the sky-high financing rate you agreed to pay.
- Showing up at a dealer without knowing your credit report. Then you are putty in the dealer's hands. He could tell you that you are "subprime" and will have to pay through the nose for a car loan (up to 23 percent) or that you're ineligible for any car loan.
- Not keeping your credit check current can also land you in a ditch. If there are errors on your report, it can take 60 days to correct them, so do not apply for any credit until all disputes are resolved and you've verified your credit score or FICO score. Close old accounts, remove old addresses and other errors from your credit report and try to get any "charge-offs" removed by negotiating with your creditors. Wait until your score goes up to 680 if you want to get the loan rate reserved for good-credit customers. Try not to apply for credit until you have been at your new job at least six months and hold off if you have moved in the last six months.

Lenders hate nomads and most verify address and income. It's good to show a previous car loan, home mortgage, and other credit extended and repaid on your record, a steady stable job, and low credit card balances. And if you've had a bankruptcy, don't apply for a car loan for at least three years.

- Trading in a car on which you still owe money can also take you off-road. If the dealer does not pay off your loan on time, the bank can charge you interest because it's your obligation. If you owe more on your car than it's worth, if you lease, or if you put down less than 20 percent, you should get gap coverage from your insurance agent, not from the dealer. He'll charge $500-$700 when you can get it for less than half that.
- Having one dealer locate your car from another dealer will often result in unexpected fees.
- Not thinking about selling the car when you're buying—especially if you usually sell or trade in a car every few years or want to buy a new car before paying off the existing one—can land you "upside down," that is, owing more on the loan than the car is worth. (Resale values can be found at online buying services such as Kelly Blue Book at kbb.com and Edmunds.com.)
- Bringing your old car to the dealer for a trade-in is certainly the easiest course but will almost never benefit you financially. Although it's rarely the best deal in town, 44 percent of us do a trade-in just for the convenience.
- Bypassing an inspection. Half of all buyers fear that the used car they're about to buy has some mechanical problem, but only one in four has it professionally inspected prior to the sale, according to Green Flag Motoring Assistance and American Express. Nearly 40 percent later discover a problem that would have nixed the sale.
- Accepting a breakdown contract. Instead, get a wear-and-tear *and* mechanical breakdown contract that covers things that wear down such as piston rings. Do not assume that everything is covered.

And make sure the warranty does not require that you have a franchised car dealer do the repairs. On the other hand, never use a repair shop that refuses to work with your warranty company. Chances are it means they'll overcharge standard repair labor hours or force extra parts on you that you don't need.

○ Buying the car at the end of the lease. First, it's likely that the end-of-lease value in your contract is higher than the actual market value. In addition, you probably face a $300 to $400 non-negotiable *purchase option fee* buried in your lease contract should you buy the car at the end of the lease. If you must have it, haggle. Tell the dealer that without your offer he or she would have to dump the vehicle at a wholesale auction.

○ Falling for an extended warranty. Extended warranties are confusing to you and profitable for the dealer. You can only get an auto warranty on vehicles up to 138,000 miles and/or up to ten model years old. You can buy "wrap warranties" for certified used cars giving comprehensive bumper-to-bumper coverage, but don't get one at the dealer. Go directly to the manufacturer if you can. But first, make sure you actually need an extended warranty. If you lease for 36 months or less, you probably don't. Do not expect a warranty to cover preexisting failures on your car and do not file a claim within the first 60 days. Warranty companies know that 90 percent of the claims filed in the first 30 days are fraudulent claims on preexisting failures that can often be proven by independent inspectors.

○ Signing on for credit disability insurance. This is supposed to make your payments if you are injured. Experts say it's not worth it, but dealers often insist you need it.

○ Signing the contract without doing the math. Once you sign, you're saying that you have read and understand all the numbers.

○ Putting nothing down. When you buy a car always put down 20 percent instead of the zero money down that dealers push. In this way you'll have equity in the car.

○ Accepting what's on the lot. You can avoid paying through the nose for options you don't want by having the dealer order a car from the factory. It takes six to twelve weeks. But save all the paperwork because the dealer could try to renegotiate the deal. Rebates may only be valid for vehicles in dealer stock.

○ Signing for a loan with prepayment penalties. You can refinance and escape an onerous auto loan—unless your loan carries prepayment penalties. Otherwise, consider trying to negotiate a new payment plan. Or you can give over the car (and loan) to a friend (who must be approved by your lender) or sell on your own (again, you'll need permission from your creditor). Do not let your creditor sell it or take possession unless absolutely necessary. But if repossession is in the cards, drive it to your lender to avoid hundreds of dollars in fees for towing and storage.

○ Falling for callback scams. Dealers can rip you off after you sign a lease by calling you weeks after you have signed the lease to note an error in your contract. Do not be fooled, however, into thinking you have to pay more or renegotiate. Dealers have no right to rescind on an existing lease contract unless you are delinquent on payments.

Before you leave the dealership, you should:

○ have the dealer sign off on a list of all defects you spot on the car.

○ verify that the Vehicle Identification Number (VIN) of the car you bought is correctly entered on the contract to avoid any bait-and-switch problems. (The VIN is located on an engraved metal strip, usually on the dashboard against the windshield.)

○ make certain there are no blank spaces on the contract. If there are, make sure they write in a $0 or "N/A."

○ if they put a dealer prep charge of $200 to $600, insist on having it removed.

- verify before you buy what your state fees are for tags and title. You don't want to pay $350 and find out later it only costs $50 for new tags.
- verify that all options you purchased are installed in the car and are itemized on the contract. The window sticker is as good as a contract for describing factory-installed equipment. Verify that the Manufacturer's Suggested Retail Price (MSRP) sticker agrees with the options the dealer is charging you for. Make sure everything is in writing.
- never buy a new car if it has no MSRP sticker.

Auto Insurance

As long as you carry at least $500,000 of insurance per person, you may want to raise the deductible (and bank the savings for emergencies) and increase your liability coverage. You can shave some money from the premium on personal injury protection, also known as medical payments coverage. Health insurance for yourself and your family, however, already covers your medical bills after an accident, so there is no need to pay twice for medical.

If you have considerable assets, consider buying an umbrella policy that would cover both your home and auto. Umbrella policies usually start at $200 to $300 a year for up to $1 million worth of coverage.

One important new trend is the use of your credit rating to set your automobile insurance rates. The logic is that people with low credit ratings have more accidents. This is yet another reason to pay attention to your credit report, something we discuss in more length in Chapter 9.

It pays to shop around. Check Bankrate.com for insurance brokerages in your area that can help you. If you call around for quotes, include a few brand name companies as well as a few independent agents who will shop more than one company for you.

If you drive an older car, consider dropping collision insurance. Understand whether your insurance will pay for brand name or generic parts to fix your car after an accident and whether you'll be limited in your choice of mechanics or body shops. If you switch insurance companies, be sure to notify your old company in writing and make sure that the new policy picks up immediately without any gap. If your old company goofs and reports to the state that you are driving without insurance, some states take steps to suspend your driver's license. If you get a warning letter from the state, address the situation immediately. Otherwise, your next routine traffic stop could be anything but routine.

Insuring your car is one of many steps that will keep the gas guzzler from guzzling what's in your wallet.

chapter nine
TAKE CREDIT—CAREFULLY

Borrow Responsibly
Understand Your Credit Report

Do you look for and switch to credit cards with lower rates? Do you check your credit report annually for accuracy? When it comes to credit cards, most Americans (80 percent according to Bankrate's survey) know that switching to a credit card with a lower interest rate is a good idea, yet one in three of us (32 percent) never bother to do it. Indeed, 29 percent say that as long as they can afford their payments, they don't worry much about the interest rates they're paying. That is akin to tossing money out the window.

Similarly, whether you are applying for a loan or credit card, knowing what your credit report says about you will determine not just whether you get it—but how much you'll pay for it. Yet Bankrate found that while 88 percent of Americans believe that it is important to check their credit report annually for accuracy, only 57 percent actually get around to doing it.

Rules of Thumb for Applying for a Credit Card

If you have an excellent credit history, you can get a card that offers rewards and carries no annual fee. Around a third of credit card customers carry rewards cards. Most of these programs award points, "dollars" or cash value based on how much you charge. The card companies make money from fees that merchants pay when you use the card and from finance charges and penalty fees that you pay.

If you don't have credit, you need to get some. Start by opening a bank account. Then apply for a few credit cards. (Department store or gas credit cards are usually more lenient than bank-issued cards like Visa or MasterCard.) If the creditor is reluctant to offer you an unsecured card, you can always get a secured one with credit limits. The security comes from a deposit that you are required to make into a savings account.

Before you accept any credit card, find out:

- if there is an introductory rate, what it is and how long it lasts.
- what your new rate will be after the introductory rate lapses.
- if there is an application fee.
- if there are processing fees, annual fees, or late fees.
- whether there is an over-the-limit fee.
- if there are any other fees, like account termination fees or balance transfer fees.
- when and how a variable rate can be changed.
- when and how a fixed rate can be changed.
- what the grace period is before interest is applied.
- how will the company inform you of any changes in your contract.
- how the company will inform you if you are about to go over your limit.

- what the consequences are if you do go over your limit.
- what the company policy is if you have trouble paying your bill.

Rules of Thumb for Checking Your Credit Report

Whether you are applying for a loan or credit, knowing what your credit report says about you will determine not just whether you get it—but how much you'll pay for it. Your FICO score is your credit score. It is named after Fair Isaac Corporation, which creates proprietary credit scoring models.

While it is fairly simple to get your FICO score or credit report, it is, perhaps, unfairly important. Half of those who applied for their credit reports found mistakes on them according to the National Credit Reporting Association. The Federal Trade Commission says it receives more complaints about credit reporting than about any other issue.

The three credit reports that matter are Equifax (800) 685-1111, Experian (888) 397-3742, and TransUnion (800) 916-8800. You should not pay more than nine dollars for a single credit report, and depending on your location and your credit history, you may be able to get your credit reports for free. If you applied for a loan and were turned down, you are entitled to a free copy of your credit report, but you must request a copy by writing the correct credit bureau within 30 days of the rejection. With your request, you should include a copy of the declined loan application. You can also get a free report if you are unemployed, planning to apply for a job in the next 60 days, receiving public welfare assistance or believe that the credit file contains mistakes resulting from fraud. By September 1, 2005, everyone will be entitled to one free credit report each year.

Credit scores range from 300 to 850, with the vast majority of people falling into the 600 to 800 range. The higher your FICO score, the better. Borrowers applying for a mortgage with FICO scores above 680 are likely to get approved for a loan with only a cursory review. Those with scores between 620 and 680 undergo a more formal investigation, while a score below 620 means that if you do get a loan, you'll probably pay through the teeth for it. These score breaks are not hard and fast, however; they are determined by each lender and can vary accordingly.

To confuse matters further, each of the three credit bureaus sells its own credit score to lenders, but the gold standard in the banking industry is the FICO score. Currently, the only place you can directly purchase all three of your FICO scores is myFICO.com. FICO scores from the individual credit bureaus are also available to consumers from www.equifax.com, www.transunion.com, and www.intersection.com.

Your FICO score is determined by five factors (each with different weights):

1. Your past payment history (35 percent). People who have paid on time in the past are a much safer bet for lenders than those who have missed some payments.
2. The way you have used credit and the amount of credit owed (30 percent). Someone who is maxed out or close to the limit on a credit card is considered riskier than a more conservative spender.
3. The length of time over which have you established credit (15 percent). People who have had credit for a long time are less risky to lenders.
4. The number of times you have asked for credit (10 percent). The fewer requests for credit cards or loans initiated over a short period, the better.

5. The types of credit you have established (10 percent). Someone with only a credit card is generally riskier than someone who has a combination of installment and revolving loans. (On installment loans, a person borrows money once and makes fixed payments until the balance is gone, while revolving borrowers make regular payments, each of which frees up more money to access.)

Knowing your credit score can help you improve your creditworthiness and negotiate for the best possible terms for very large transactions. This is why it's critical to obtain your score three to six months before applying for a mortgage or car loan.

You can get a free estimate of your FICO credit score by using a free calculator on Bankrate. Developed with the FICO score experts at Fair Isaac, this tool lets you determine a range of what your score may be and is handy for "what if" scenarios. Check it out at www.bankrate.com/fico.

You can improve your credit score by:

- paying your bills on time.
- keeping your outstanding debt far below your credit limit.
- maintaining a long credit history.
- taking on new credit sparingly.

The Equal Credit Opportunity Act requires that if you are denied credit, the creditor must tell you the specific reasons for the denial, such as "Your income is low" or "You haven't been employed long enough." You cannot be unreasonably denied credit for not meeting "our minimum standards" or "not receiving enough points on our credit scoring system." If you were rejected because you are too near the limits on your charge cards, you may want to reapply after paying down your balances.

If you have been denied credit. or failed to get the rate or terms you want, find out if a credit scoring system was used to determined your credit score and what characteristics or factors were used in that system. Be sure to review the specific reasons in the denial letter as to why you were declined.

If you have made mistakes in paying previous loans, bounced checks, made late payments, or had other credit problems, you may still be able to reduce the amount of damage to your credit score with explanations. Make sure the facts on a credit report are correct.

How Vulnerable Are You?

In 2003, 9.9 million Americans were victims of identity theft, according to the Federal Trade Commission. Over the last five years, this figure is more than 27 million. The crime is no longer limited to stealing a victim's personal information and using it to obtain a credit card, cell phone, and so on in the victim's name—now identity thieves are even obtaining mortgages and medical care.

The reason, of course, is that there is a welter of personal information available out there—and it's easier for banks and corporations to write off a loss than it is to prosecute it. According to identity theft expert Frank Abagnale—the one-time conman profiled in the movie *Catch Me If You Can*—most district attorneys will not pursue cases under $5,000, most U.S. attorneys will not prosecute white-collar crimes under $250,000 and the FBI will not investigate crimes under $100,000. And the problem of identity theft is only likely to intensify. Short of buying a criss-cross shredder (straight-line shredders are too easy for criminals to decode), you should balance your bank statement and demand that your credit bureau alert you if anyone is checking your credit history.

Most people believe that identity theft insurance protects them— that if a thief drains their account of $5,000, they'll get that money back. They won't. You are only reimbursed for out-of-pocket expenses incurred to the problem fixed—what it costs to take time off from work to make phone calls, write letters, and so on—but not the actual loss from identity theft.

The scams are so inventive that it's easy to see why identity theft is such a burgeoning business. One scam, for example, asks you to pay $100 a month for daily updates on a family member serving in the military. Another gets you to think you're paying off a debt—on a canceled Visa card. In another you discover that you're a victim of the advance- fee scam. Some scammers send out legitimate-looking emails that claim to be from a company you do business with reporting an account error, possible fraud, or other problem with the account. Sometimes the emails claim that your credit card has been charged for pornogra- phy and they need you to verify the information by clicking on a link and entering account information on the linked Website. The link takes you to a fake Website that gathers information that could be used to drain your bank accounts and charge up your credit cards.

Student Credit Cards

In a practice not quite as wicked as identity theft but sometimes just as perilous, credit card companies woo college students. In the past, issuers courted college graduates; now they are soliciting 18-year- olds—and even younger teens—who tend to see credit cards as "free money," since their parents are footing the bills. Many are unaware how quickly charges can add up.

More than half of all college freshmen (54 percent) carry a credit card. By sophomore year, that number rises to 92 percent. 47 percent of college students have four or more credit cards, according to a 2001 study by Nellie Mae, a national provider of higher education loans.

Credit card issuers make it so easy for a college student to qualify for a card; the issuers realize that parents can be counted on to bail out their children who have run up oversized balances or fall behind in payments. Credit card issuers also want college students as customers because students tend to be loyal to their first credit card; they'll keep on charging on the card long after graduation.

Used well, credit cards can play an important role for college students. They teach financial responsibility and ease the way into the postgraduate financial world. But credit cards can also leave you financially bruised with wounds that will not heal until long after the diploma has yellowed on the wall.

Today, more than one in five (21 percent) of undergraduates who have cards have high-level balances (between $3,000 and $7,000). This is 61 percent more than the number of students who had such high balances in 2000. From the time they arrive on campus to when they graduate, students double their average credit card debt and triple the number of cards in their wallets, according to Nellie Mae.

To find the best terms on a student card, click on credit cards at Bankrate.com. Most student cards come with starting credit lines ranging from $500 to $1,000. In our latest survey, interest rates on student credit cards range from 10 percent to 19.8 percent. These rates are not as good as what's available for adults with good credit, but not as bad as what's offered to people who have already mishandled credit. All of the ones at the low end of the scale are variable-rate cards, so you can expect them to rise. (We're in an environment of very low rates right now.)

If you find yourself buried in credit card debt, take a moment to assess the damage. List all creditors, noting balances, credit lines, interest rates, and monthly payments. Then track expenses. How much money comes in and how much goes out each month? Where is it going and why? Are there places you can scale back spending and free up more money for paying down card debt? Then you must Immediately stop charging on credit cards. Pay with cash or debit cards instead. At the same time, pay down the card balances to zero by dealing with one card at a time. Pay $25, $50, $100, or whatever you can spare on top of the minimum payment. Minimize interest costs by transferring balances to the card with the lowest interest rate. From a dollars-and-cents standpoint, it is best to pay down the card with the highest interest rate first. Once that first balance is paid off, focus on the card with the next highest interest rate and so on.

If you have been a good card customer and always paid your bills on time, you may want to call your issuer and ask for a lower rate. Many times card companies will, if pressed, cut a break for a student because they want to keep the young debtor as a cardholder for life. A student who slips up once on a card payment, for example, may be able get a late fee waived with one quick phone call. It is certainly worth a shot.

If you are way over your head in debt, talk to a credit counselor from a Consumer Credit Counseling Service. There are about 1,400 of them across the United States. Credit counseling is in large enough demand that there is an office near most large college campuses.

It's also a good idea for students to talk to their parents. Students on campus today are inundated with card offers, many giving away free hats and T-shirts for simply filling out an application. Credit card applications are stacked near bulletin boards or are stuffed into students bags when they buy books. So the pressure is there. Parents can counter it somewhat by talking to their children about money and about wisely handling debt before they head off to campus. They should set rules about responsible credit card usage and warn their children of the pitfalls of improper use of credit. Recognize that one or two low-limit cards is enough. You must stay within your credit limit and should avoid using credit cards for small purchases such as sodas and snacks. You should never use your card to secure a cash advance (there is an upfront fee of two to four percent on the amount you withdraw and you'll be stuck paying a whopper of an interest rate with no grace period) and you should pay your bills on time every month.

Despite the dangers of debt, college students should not spurn credit cards. Graduating from college without a credit card may be as bad an idea as graduating without a diploma. Just as a degree establishes your rite of passage and mastery of a subject, a college student who uses a credit card well establishes himself or herself as a credit-worthy individual. Without a credit history, you cannot rent a car or get a good car insurance policy. You could get turned down for an apartment when a potential landlord checks your credit history and finds nothing there—or you could be asked to shell out an enormous deposit before moving in.

Once you graduate, getting a credit card will be a lot tougher and the credit card offers less forthcoming. And if a preapproved credit card offer does comes your way, there is an excellent chance that you'll be turned down because of a lack of revolving credit on your credit report. Study the terms and costs of any offer before signing on.

The following five questions anyone should ask about a credit card:

1. Does the card have an annual fee? There is no reason to pay one. Avoid cards that charge them.
2. What is the card's annual percentage rate (APR)? The lower the interest rate, the less money you'll pay when you carry a balance.
3. Does the card comes with a super-low introductory rate? If so, how long will that teaser rate last? Try to pay off your card balance before the teaser rate expires.

4. How long is the card's grace period? Most cards offer grace periods to customers that pay off their balances each month. A grace period is the time after a purchase is made (or from the end of the billing cycle) during which interest is not charged. If payment is made in full by the end of the grace period, no interest is charged. But if only a partial payment is made, interest kicks in at the end of the grace period. Many issuers have whittled down the interest-free grace periods on credit cards from 25 days to 20. Some credit cards have no grace periods at all, which means the interest clock starts ticking after each and every purchase. Avoid them.

5. What are the card's penalty policies? While you may not plan to miss a credit card payment or go over the limit, it is important to realize what will happen if you do. Penalty rates and fees are on the rise. Some card issuers' policies are punitive, so be sure to check. Pay careful attention to what will happen if you pay late during a card's introductory period. Will that super-low teaser rate disappear after one little mistake?

Don't overlook credit cards available from credit unions. These cards tend to have more consumer-friendly rates and fees.

chapter ten

DEALING WITH DEBT

Borrowing Responsibly
Credit Card Bill of Rights

Do you make more than the minimum payments on your credit cards? The two issues that Bankrate's survey said were most important were paying bills on time and making more than the minimum payments on credit cards. And for the great majority who felt these issues were most important, many carried through and did it. However, 27 percent sometimes pay just the minimum on their credit card, and this chapter is for them.

Borrowing—at the best rates and what you can afford to pay back —to buy a home or pay college tuition usually makes good sense and establishes a healthy credit history. But people in debt are like gluttons at a buffet who eat without thinking of their waistlines and the price they'll have to pay the next day. More than half of those in debt —52 percent—blame their predicament on poor money management and ignorance about financial protocols.

Nowadays, there are more credit cards in America than there are television sets. Almost as many people carry them as have a driver's license. The average cardholder has three to four bank cards and a total of eight to ten credit cards. Twenty-three percent of American households now have at least one debit card. Over 65 percent have credit cards as have valid passports. Just nine percent of American adults do not have at least one major credit card.

Plastic is definitely a financial convenience. But too many people abuse it. This is partly why 17 percent of Americans are deep in debt, with little hope of climbing out of the hole. A fifth describes their financial position as precarious. Collectively, we owe more than $2.016 trillion in nonmortgage debt—roughly equal to $7,000 for every man, woman, and child in the country.

Bankrate studied the level of stress all this credit card debt is causing us, and the results are not surprising. Seventy-four percent of Americans are very concerned about being able to pay their credit card bills, even though 58 percent claim to pay their bills in full every month. This high level of concern is consistent across people who scored high and low on our financial literacy test.

Having up to four cards is permissible—as long as you have a reason for all of them. A Visa, MasterCard, and Discover card for personal use allow you to take advantages of promotions you would otherwise miss and purchase from outlets that don't take all three. You might want a separate card just for business and a fallback card. More than that and you're inviting an unhealthy urge to splurge.

The average American household has over $8,000 in credit card debt. This means that with credit card interest rates averaging around 18 percent (1.5 percent on the unpaid balance monthly), Americans pay $1,400 per household in interest a year. This is a steep price to pay for convenience and one reason why eight percent of families have missed a debt payment by two months in a recent year, according to the Federal Reserve. Twenty-three percent have been contacted by a collection agency for a late bill. And more than one million in a recent year declared bankruptcy.

If you make $2,200 a month and you spend $440 or more of that toward credit cards and a car payment, you're heading for a financial noose. At Bankrate, we recommend a maximum of 20 percent of your gross income as the ceiling for unsecured debt and installment loan payments. If you don't know the annual percentage rate (APR), fees, grace periods and other key costs of your cards, you're probably paying through the nose.

Don't jeopardize your credit rating by overdrawing your bank account or by missing or being tardy with payments to any creditor. Do not allow anyone else access to your credit card, debit card, or bank account. Do not give your card number to anyone over the phone or Internet unless you have initiated the transaction. And avoid cash advances. You'll pay an upfront fee of two to four percent of the total amount (or at least $10) you withdraw and you'll be stuck paying an excessive interest rate, often close to 20 percent. And because there is no grace period on a cash advance, the interest charges will begin to mount as soon as the money comes out of the ATM. Some banks even charge you if you carry an inactive card or call their toll-free number to check your balance.

Use cash to pay for meals, vacations and other "perishables" if you're not regularly paying off your monthly bill. Save for something costly that you really want before putting it on plastic to make sure that you can pay the balance when it's due, thereby avoiding interest charges.

Get rid of the cards you don't need. Cancel them if there's no balance on them or if you plan to take out a mortgage or car loan in the coming months where you need to show creditworthiness. However, closing unused credit cards right before applying for a loan might adversely affect your credit score if your debt-to-available-credit ratio rises. (Then pay them down instead.) Phone each creditor for instructions on how to close your account. Keep a record of whom you spoke with and ask him or her to record the call so that the company has a record of your request, too. Be prepared for a sales pitch to get you to keep the card. Make sure the accounts that were closed are listed as "closed by cardholder request." If you prefer, use one of the Bankrate form letters in the Appendix to close your account.

Only as a last option should you consider a debt consolidation loan. The most important thing is to get your spending under control (see Chapter 3, "Your Inner Spending Demon.") But make sure that the costs of the new, bundled loan actually shave something off what you're already paying various creditors. If not, bankruptcy may be a better option. You could also consider using a financial counselor or debt manager to negotiate with your creditors to arrange a repayment schedule. They may be able to lower the interest rate on your credit cards. But understand that even nonprofit counseling organizations charge a fee for their services. In 2003 1.6 million American households voluntarily sought counseling for debt, according to the National Foundation for Consumer Credit. The average debtor seeking help from a counseling service owes more than $20,000.

Debtors tend to be in denial. Confirmation of deep debt denial emerged when Bankrate asked people if they would be willing to admit to a friend how much they owe on credit cards. Only 54 percent said yes, fewer than would be willing to come clean about their weight, age, rent, or income...and the only thing more personal involved details of their love life!

A professional debt manager will help you take an honest look at what you owe—and force you to stop racking up debt. It is a good idea to verify certifications or third-party registrations with the Association of Independent Consumer Credit Counseling Agencies or the National Foundation of Credit Counseling. You should also ask for (and check) references.

Your Credit Card Bill of Rights

Have you ever been charged for something you didn't buy? Have you ever been charged the wrong amount? The Fair Credit Billing Act has made it easy to get an error on your credit card statement fixed. You need to mail a written complaint of the error on your bill within 60 days from when your issuer mailed your billing statement to "Billing Inquiries," which is listed on the back of your card bill. (This is *not* the same as the address for payments.) It's best to send a dispute letter via certified mail, and request a return receipt. Include your name, address, account number, and a description of the problem. If you have anything to back up your claim, include that (such as a copy of a return receipt).

Once a credit card issuer receives your dispute letter, it is required to act within two billing cycles (no longer than 90 days) and acknowledge your complaint in writing within 30 days. During this time your card company may not take any action to collect the disputed amount; you are allowed to withhold payment on the disputed charge. Once the investigation is finished, the card issuer will either credit your account (including any finance charges or late fees related to the disputed charge) or notify you that the disputed charge is correct. You then have at least ten days to pay the charge or to reassert your dispute in writing. Your credit report may suffer, however. It will list the charge as a delinquent payment, with the addendum that you believe that you do not owe the money in question.

You also have the right to withhold payment on damaged or poor-quality merchandise purchased for more than $50 within your home state or 100 miles of your home address with a credit card. The caveat is that you must make a real "good faith attempt" at resolving the dispute with a merchant before you can ask your issuer to stop a credit card payment. Keep a record of what was said.

Late Fees and Why You Should Avoid Them

To increase their profits, some credit card issuers have shortened interest-free grace periods from 25 days to 20, and increased late fees. As a result, customers have less time to pay off balances and more time to be charged late fees and interest when they don't pay in full. Being late on credit card payments is very costly. Late fees can be as much as $39 each. To avoid them you must follow precisely your card issuer's payment guidelines outlined on the back of each credit card bill—including sending it to a specific payment address at a specific time. Many issuers say payment must be received in the morning to be credited that day; they stipulate that payments must arrive in the preprinted envelope sent.

While the Fair Credit Billing Act requires issuers to credit payments the day they are received, each issuer is allowed to set specific payment guidelines. If any of the guidelines are not met, the issuer can take as many as five days to credit the payment. This means that a timely payment could easily become "late" during this five-day period. You should always:

- use the preprinted envelope provided by the credit card company.
- include the billing coupon and write the amount being paid in the box provided.
- be sure that checks are legible and signed, the credit card account number appears on the check, and the payment amount is correct.
- send payment with proper postage to the payment address requested by the issuer. Mail your payment at least one week in advance of the due date.

It's best to pay the bill as soon as it arrives—even if you only make the two percent minimum payment.

- You could ask to move your due date to right after payday—not when all your other bills become due.
- Consider setting up automatic, online payments. You can sign up for these services on issuer Websites. Choose an online payment amount that automatically covers the minimum amount due on a credit card each month and an automatic payment date well in advance of your credit card due date. To keep your interest costs down, make additional card payments online or by snail mail as soon as you can.
- Consider paying by phone using the toll-free number on the back of your credit card. You must provide a check number and the bank routing number (printed at the bottom of every check). After you hang up, rip up the check because you will not be able to use it again. Some issuers charge fees, ranging from $5 to $15 for this service. Be sure to ask.
- If the due date is soon, consider sending a credit card payment by express mail or wiring the payment via Western Union. The U.S. Postal Service currently charges $13.65 for an express mail envelope which guarantees next-day delivery by noon to most destinations. Wiring your payment will cost you as well. Western Union's fees for money-wiring service vary depending upon the amount of payment. These express services, while costly, are still cheaper than most credit card late fees. Make sure you send your express payment to the proper address. Many issuers have separate payment addresses for express payments. The last thing you want to do is slow the processing of an express payment by sending it to the wrong address.
- If you are charged a late fee even though you mailed your payment well before the due date, call and ask your issuer to waive the fee. Many will do so as a courtesy to customers with good payment records. If not, consider getting a card from a smaller issuer such as a credit union or a local community bank. These tend to be more

lenient when it comes to penalty fees. Late fees at community banks range from $10 to $15. Community banks also accept card payments 10 to 15 days after due dates without penalties. Credit unions generally accept a card payment ten days after a due date without penalty. And if a credit union should charge you a late fee, it will only be $10.50 on average. However, many credit unions and community banks have credit cards issued by third-party issuers such as MBNA and carry the same fee policies you find anywhere else.

Every credit card company has different criteria for pricing card accounts. When the card issuer merges with another or is taken over, the low interest rate you've been paying can become history in the blink of an eye. Similarly, late fees and grace periods can change overnight. The law requires issuers give customers just 15 days notice. Card customers have seen their interest rates rise when their card issuer moved headquarters to a state that has no cap.

chapter eleven
APRIL 15 BLUES

Manage Your Withholding Better

Use Tax Deductions and Credits

Do you adjust your W-4 form annually to make sure you're not giving the government too much money? More than half of Americans say that it is very important to adjust their W-4 forms annually, yet Bankrate discovered that just 39 percent of them do it. These people are lending the government money at zero percent interest! This is hardly the only error Americans make when dealing with the Internal Revenue Service.

If there is any prime season for financial stress, it's April: tax time. It's not just that taxes mean shelling out your hard-earned money—the average American paid $5,497 in taxes in 2002, according to the Tax Foundation, though 69 percent usually get a refund—it's that preparing them means lots of work. And it is work that we're not entirely sure we're doing right. In fact, only 42 percent of Americans are confident that they fill out their tax forms properly. A nervous ten percent confess that they haven't got the foggiest idea of what they're doing.

Although the Internal Revenue Service audits fewer than two percent of the returns it receives (and won't disclose precisely how it targets those unfortunates), the possibility of facing the tax man is traumatic. More people would rather take their chances in a car crash—assuming no one's hurt—than be hit by an IRS audit. Thirteen percent would even rather undergo root canal surgery than be subjected to IRS scrutiny, according to Bernice Kanner's book *Are You Normal About Money?*

Slightly more than half of Americans do their own taxes. The IRS estimates that it takes a taxpayer 35.8 hours to fill out a Form 1040 and Schedules A through D, up from 30.6 hours five years ago and 28.6 hours in 1989. Even some tax lawyers and accountants admit that they're stumped by some of the new tax regulations and forms. It's no wonder we want to put off doing our taxes. Still, most Americans file their taxes on time. Just 1.6 percent admit that they are usually a few days late. Nine percent almost always get an extension, giving themselves an extra four months to complete their returns. Getting an extension just allows you to delay the paperwork—not the payment of taxes, which are due on April 15 even if you do not file the forms.

Putting off a tax payment won't make it go away. It will still be there, accruing penalties until you get to it. You must file a tax return in the United States if you've earned money and you're an American citizen. You must also file if you owe payroll taxes on unreported tips or other reported income that wasn't collected, if you are liable for any alternative minimum tax, or if you owe taxes on individual retirement accounts, Archer MSA accounts, or an employer-sponsored retirement plan. You must file a return if you receive advance payments for the earned income credit from your employer, if your net earnings from self-employment are $400 or more, or if you earn employee income of at least $108.28 from either a church or qualified church-controlled organization that is exempt from employer-paid FICA and Medicare taxes.

There are three levels of income to consider when calculating your taxes: total income, adjusted gross income, and taxable income. Total income is the sum of all sources of income including wages, salaries, tips, interest and dividends, capital gains, Social Security benefits, and money earned outside the country. Subtracting from that all allowed above-the-line adjustments gives you what is called adjusted gross income (AGI). Taking away all allowed deductions and exemptions equals your taxable income. Allowable deductions may include contributions to your IRA, interest on student loans used to pay for qualified educational expenses, alimony payments, retirement and health insurance–related expenses if you are self-employed, and moving expenses if related to taking a new job.

When you file a federal income tax return, you take either a standard deduction or you can itemize deductions—whichever gives you the advantage. Your standard deduction is the amount to deduct from your AGI in order to calculate your taxable income. The larger the deduction, the lower your taxable income and the smaller the amount you'll owe in taxes. The IRS increases the standard deduction each year to adjust for inflation. The standard deduction is likely to be close to what your itemized deductions would be, on average, and is much easier to calculate.

If you do choose to itemize, you can deduct:

- the mortgage interest you pay each year up to $1 million in home-acquisition debt and $100,000 in home-equity debt.
- the taxes you pay to your state and local tax authority.
- qualified medical and dental expenses that exceed 7.5 percent of your adjusted gross income.
- charitable contributions.

○ miscellaneous expenses related to your job, such as travel, lodging, or meals as long as they exceed two percent of your AGI.

You can claim exemptions for yourself and for each dependent. As a general rule, you can claim at least one exemption for each person in your household.

Better than a tax deduction or personal exemption is a tax credit. It reduces the amount of taxes you owe dollar for dollar. With deductions and exemptions, you get a certain percentage back depending on your tax bracket.

Major categories of tax credits include:

○ Earned income credit, aimed at reducing the tax burden on lower-income taxpayers.
○ Saver's tax credit for lower-income workers who contribute to qualified retirement plans.
○ Child-related tax credits, which include child and dependent care expenses for children under 14, child tax credit, and adoption credit. For 2003, the maximum child tax credit per child was $1,000.

When you invest in the stock market you may wind up owing capital gains taxes on the profits from the sale of those investments. If you sell at a lower price than what you paid, you earn a capital loss. The amount of capital gain is calculated by subtracting the basis—what the stock was worth when you bought it—from the price for which you sell the asset. You generally add the costs to buy the asset to your basis.

How long you hold your investment determines whether your capital gain is treated as a long- or short-term gain. If you hold a capital asset for more than one year (366 days), the capital gain you realize on its sale is considered a long-term capital gain. Otherwise it's a short-term capital gain and is taxed as ordinary income instead of the lower rates accorded long-term gains.

In addition to capital gains, stock dividends generate taxable income. Beginning in 2003, dividends have been taxed at the same rate as capital gains. Distributed short-term capital gains on mutual funds are taxed as ordinary income and distributed dividends and long-term capital gains are taxed as long-term capital gains. When you sell shares of a mutual fund for a higher price than you paid, you pay either a short- or long-term capital gains tax, depending on how long you have owned the shares.

The IRS allows you to offset your capital gains with capital losses, but bans investors from selling a security to lock in a capital loss, then buying it back at a lower price within 30 days.

You may be subject to the Alternative Minimum Tax (AMT), which was created in 1969 to ensure that wealthy taxpayers did not use loopholes to avoid paying their fair share. Back then, fewer than 200 filers avoided paying any federal taxes. Now, more than 3 million taxpayers could face the AMT and the number is growing. The starting point for figuring any AMT is your regular taxable income. From there, some of the deductions you claim are added back (tax-preference items) and then a special exemption amount is subtracted. The result is subject to the alternative tax. You may be subject to the ATM if your annual taxable income is more than $58,000 and you are married (filing a joint return) or if your annual earnings top $40,250 and you are filing as single or head of household.

What You Can Do to Get Ready for Tax Time

o Check and adjust your paycheck withholding to make sure you have enough taxes taken out of your paycheck—especially if you married, had a child, bought a house, or are expecting a large bonus at the end of the year. Otherwise you could end up owing the Internal Revenue Service more in penalties and interest. Compare this year's current pay stub to last year's. If too much tax is being taken out, you can increase exemptions on your W-4 to reduce withholding. If too little is being withheld, direct your company to take out an additional, specific dollar amount in taxes from your remaining paychecks.

o Make your January 1 mortgage payment (which really represents interest for the month of December) before the end of the year so that you can take an additional deduction this tax year for the interest paid. The same early-bird approach also applies to deductible property taxes. If your county or municipal tax collector will take your tax payment (or part of it) in December, it will accelerate your tax benefits. Consider paying estimated income taxes in December instead of the January due date to shift the tax benefit into the current year.

o You may benefit from the recent law which cut the capital gains rate to 15 percent and reduced taxes on dividends from the ordinary income rate to 15 percent. You can help your tax situation even more by selling poorly performing stocks at a loss to balance out any gains. And you can use up an additional $3,000 in capital losses to reduce taxable ordinary income. If your bad stocks cost you more, you can carry the excess into future tax years. (But you'll have to wait more than 30 days to buy the stocks back, or be subject to IRS penalty.)

o Get philanthropic. Itemized gifts of cash or goods can be deducted to reduce your tax liability. Consider donating some stock, especially one you've held for a while that's struggling to gain value in the current market. This way you can deduct the current market value of your stock gift before it drops any lower. You also can deduct charitable travel, at 14 cents per mile, if you used your vehicle to do volunteer work.

○ Don't forget that you may give up to $11,000 (cash or property) to each child or grandchild every year without being subject to the federal gift tax. Your spouse can do the same, bringing your limit up to $22,000.

○ The IRS does not let you count medical deductions unless they exceed 7.5 percent of your adjusted gross income; however, if you're nearing this figure it's a good time to consider that elective surgery to bump your medical bills up to the deductibility threshold. One caveat: There must be a solid medical reason for the procedure. You can also include any dependent's medical treatments, the installation costs of special, doctor-prescribed therapeutic equipment, medically necessary improvements to your home, and travel for medical treatments at 12 cents per mile.

○ Pay up your union or professional dues, tax preparation and investment advisory fees, legal and accounting fees, job-related equipment and educational expenses, or subscriptions to business publications on December 31st and you can use them to cut your taxes, as long as they cumulatively exceed two percent of your adjusted income. If you're near the threshold in December, prepay some of these expenses. Buy the uniform you were going to get in January, extend your business journal subscription another year, and pay the registration fee for a job-related computer class that you plan to take in February.

○ If you have a flexible spending account with money still in it and it operates on a calendar basis, make your medical appointments to use it. And if you haven't started a retirement savings account, do so. If you already have one, add to it. In many cases, you get an immediate tax break and begin building a nest egg sooner.

○ The most overlooked credit is child or dependent care credit. This is followed by education credits, mortgage interest and charitable gift deductions as well as miscellaneous expenses. These include things such as tax preparation fees, job-hunting expenses, the fee for a safe-deposit box, a variety of work-related expenses, and gambling losses.

○ Hold on to your returns and supporting documentation for seven years, after which time you cannot be audited.

The Alternative Minimum Tax

When you complete an individual income tax return you will have to complete a worksheet to determine whether you owe the Alternative Minimum Tax. If you do, you must complete a special form (Form 6251). The tax rate for the AMT is 26 percent of the first $175,000 of ordinary income that exceeds a certain exempt amount of income. The income that exceeds the exemption amount is the AMT. The tax rate increases to 28 percent for higher incomes.

If you're employed, your employer is required to withhold federal income (FIT) and Federal Insurance Contribution Act (FICA) taxes from your salary or wages. FICA taxes include payments for Social Security and Medicare. The number of allowances you claim when you complete a W-4 form, together with any additional dollar amount, determines the rate at which FIT is withheld from your paycheck. You can submit a new W-4 with your employer at any time or change your number of dependents. You want to estimate as well as you can so that your total amount withheld for the year equals what you owe. Too much withheld, and you get a refund—with the government using your money to earn interest that you could be earning. Too little withheld, and you have to pony up—with penalties, too, if you have not paid at least 90 percent of your tax liability for the year by January 15.

Your employer, using tables supplied by the government, determines how much of your paycheck should be withheld based on information you provided on the W-4 form you filled out when you started work. It can (and should) be amended any time circumstances in your life change (you marry, become parents, dependent, you take on a mortgage, and so on) to make sure you're not giving the government too much money. Each allowance reduces the taxes withheld and increases your take-home pay. You should try to withhold at least 90 percent of what you think you'll owe for that year, but not much more or you'll have effectively given the government an interest-free loan.

Each January, your employer sends you and the IRS a Form W-2 that reports your earnings for the prior tax year and the total amount of tax you had withheld. You are then responsible for calculating how much more you owe and paying the difference by April 15, or figuring out how much the IRS should refund you if you overpaid.

If you are self-employed, expect to have a lot of investment income, are selling property in a given tax year, or do not have enough taxes withheld from your paycheck to cover all your earnings, you'll probably need to pay estimated taxes quarterly (April 15, June 15, September 15, and January 15). If, after taking all your deductions, exemptions and credits, you do not think you will owe any more than $1,000 on April 15 on top of what you've already paid in taxes for the year, then you are not required to pay estimated taxes.

Even if you don't have the cash to pay your tax bill, file your return on time to avoid the IRS failure-to-file penalty of five percent per month (up to a maximum of 25 percent) of your balance due. Of course, you can file an extension that gives you until September 15 to file. But if you owe the government money, the penalties will accrue and it will cost you more.

You might want to put some or all of your entire tax bill on an American Express, Discover, MasterCard, or Visa card and file through www. officialpayments.com, www.turbotax.com, or www.link2Gov.com. But while this may get you off the hook with Uncle Sam, it will cost you generally 2.5 percent of your tax bill plus interest charges if you do not pay off your credit card in full. If you owe a king's ransom, the IRS is willing to accept installment payments. You even get to pick your monthly payment amount and the day it will be due as long as you pay off the due tax in at least three years. The IRS charges a one-time fee of $43 to process the payment plan; it adds penalties and interest to your unpaid tax bill. But if your return was filed on time and you applied for the payment program before you got a levy notice, the penalty drops from 0.5 percent of the balance due each month to 0.25 percent when the IRS approves your request.

If you cannot pay your tax bill off in several years, it's time to negotiate. Offer the IRS a lump sum payment less than the total amount of tax you owe. Your chances of having it accepted are better if the amount reasonably reflects your ability to pay—not your skill at haggling. There is a $150 application fee to discourage this practice. If approved, the $150 goes toward your new payment amount.

Even when we get a refund, few of us actually like filing our tax returns. First, the process of collecting all the necessary filing information takes up our precious time. Then there's the actual filling out of forms. Finally, there's the worry—sometimes warranted, sometimes not—that we're going to get "caught" by the Internal Revenue Service.

But perhaps the worst part of tax filing is that the whole process tends to make most of us feel like fools! People with advanced educational degrees tremble when confronted by 1040s, depreciation formulas, and deductibility guidelines. In fact, during tax season most of us become adopted brothers and sisters of hapless Homer Simpson. We find ourselves making silly tax mistakes, slapping our foreheads, and muttering "D'oh!"

Unfortunately, when it comes to taxes, that "D'oh!" can cost dough. Sometimes an error means paying more in taxes. Other times it delays refunds. To help make sure your return is perfect, here are 16 common tax-filing errors that you can avoid.

1. Misfiguring the child tax credit. The good intentions of lawmakers have turned into a tax-filing nightmare for more than a million tax-payers. Last year, the popular child tax credit was increased from $600 to $1,000. Rather than make parents wait until they filed their returns this year to get the added tax break, the IRS was instructed to send out the extra money last summer. Now taxpayers who claim the credit must take any advance payment into account on their 1040 or 1040A forms.

   Be sure to use the worksheet in your tax return instruction book to calculate the proper credit amount. If you don't, you can be sure that the IRS will catch the mistake and refigure your taxes for you. This means that your refund be less than you expected; in addition, the added time it take the IRS to correct your filing means the refund will get to you later.
2. Making math errors. Every year, the most common mistake on tax returns is bad math. Mistakes in arithmetic or in transferring figures from one schedule to another will get you an immediate correction notice. Math errors also can reduce your tax refund or result in you owing more tax than you thought.
3. Not including Social Security numbers. Since the IRS stopped putting taxpayer Social Security numbers on tax package labels in response to privacy concerns, many taxpayers forget to write in their identification numbers. Your tax ID number is crucial because so many transactions—income statements, savings account interest, retirement plan contributions—are keyed to this number. The number also is vital to claim tax credits you apply for, such as the Child Tax and Additional Child Tax credits and ones for educational

expenses and dependent care costs. Without the numbers, or with wrong ones, the IRS may disallow these tax breaks.

4. Not signing and dating your return. For legal purposes, the IRS will not process a return if it does not have a signature. If you prefer, file electronically using your own privately selected personal identification number; this serves as an electronic signature.

5. Not using the preprinted label and envelope from the tax package. Use the preprinted label and envelope for your tax return, so the folks at the IRS will be able to easily and accurately read your personal information. It is not a way for the agency to more easily track and audit you—honest! In fact, if you're expecting a refund, you will probably get it sooner if you use the label.

6. Forgetting about interest and dividends. Thanks to your Social Security number on bank and investment accounts, the IRS pretty much knows how much unearned income you made as soon as you do. If you forget to include this information on your return, the IRS examiners will let you know that you owe taxes on it, too. So don't give the IRS the chance to send you a notice about absent income, or it could cost you penalty and interest charges. Plus, reporting this money is now easier, since you can make up to $1,500 in unearned income before you have to file Schedule B.

7. Forgetting to claim charitable donations. Did you give to charitable groups last year? All types of donations—cash, clothing, household items, and even cars—could be valuable tax deductions, so make sure you count them all when you file. Be sure to follow the donation tax rules, the most important being that you give to a qualified organization, that is, one that has tax-exempt status with the IRS. And if you didn't get around to dropping off your excess goods at your favorite charity in time to claim them on your current return, don't despair. Do it now and file away your contribution records so you can use them when you file next year.

8. Not including all your forms. Do not forget to attach your W-2 form, so the IRS can confirm the wage amount you report on your return. If it was a complicated tax year requiring a lot of additional forms to support your 1040, make sure that the extra work is not wasted—get those forms in with your return, too.

9. Not properly tracking your investment basis. Calculating capital gains on stocks and funds involves several complicated steps. One that you cannot afford to mess up is figuring what your stocks cost you—called the basis—before you sold them. If your investment paid dividends or capital gains distributions that you reinvested in the stock or fund, you paid tax on them in the year they were earned. These amounts should be added to your cost basis to ensure that you do not double pay tax money to Uncle Sam when you sell them.

10. Using the EZ form when a longer form could cut your taxes. If you opt for the 1040EZ way when filing your return, you could pay more taxes than you should. If your tax life is not that complicated, filling out a longer form might not take much time at all. You are not required to fill out every line—just the ones that apply to you. And the longer 1040A and 1040 forms give you several opportunities to cut your taxable income, such as subtracting student loan interest, contributions to a deductible IRA, and alimony payments made. This means less tax to pay. So take a few extra minutes to see which form fits your filing needs; it could help you pocket more tax cash.

11. Making the check out incorrectly—or forgetting to sign it! If you owe money and choose to pay by check, make it payable to the United States Treasury, not the IRS. This change safeguards your check a bit more. Otherwise, a few pen strokes could turn "IRS" into "I.R. Smith" and your check could end up being cashed by a thief. And don't forget to sign it. This payment-delaying technique will not sit well with the taxman and it could cost you more. If the

tax collector has to send your check back to you for a signature, you could miss the filing deadline and end up owing penalties and interest.

12. Forgetting to group your deductions. Many deductions—medical costs, miscellaneous expenses—are allowed only if you reach a certain amount, so you might need to shift, or group, some of these costs into one tax year to take advantage. This can be as simple as prepaying professional magazine subscriptions or opting for an elective medical procedure in a tax year in which you're near the deductibility requirements.

13. Not taking all the credits you're eligible for. Do not pass up any opportunities for getting a tax credit—it could mean money in your pocket! There are many credits available, including ones for education costs, child and dependent care expenses, and the earned income credit that could totally erase a tax bill and even give lower-salaried taxpayers a refund. Check out Bankrate.com's "tax basics" area for details about credits to see if you qualify for any of them.

14. Using the wrong tax table. Are you positive that the amount of tax you have calculated is right? It is easy to make a mistake reading the tax tables listed in the back of the tax return instruction booklets. The print is small, and there are a lot of figures on the pages. Make sure you use the correct column for your filing status. Each status owes a different tax amount in every taxable income range, and it could make a big difference in your tax bill or refund.

Using any tax table could be an even costlier mistake for some taxpayers. Were all of your long-term capital gains from mutual fund distributions, letting you simply report them directly on your form 1040 or 1040A? Sure, this means you have no extra forms to file. But you do have some additional figuring to ensure that you do not overpay your taxes. Compute your tax using the worksheet in your return's instruction booklet. It will let you benefit from the lower long-term capital gains rate, now 15 percent for most filers. If you do not figure your IRS bill this way, you'll end up paying taxes on your investment earnings at your regular income tax rate—as much as 35 percent on 2003 returns.

15. Missing the deadline to request an extension. Missing the April deadline for filing your return is not the end of the world, but it may mean paying a late filing penalty and interest fees. If you just cannot finish your tax paperwork this spring, you can get four extra months by asking for more time. Just make sure you submit Form 4868 (Application for Automatic Extension of Time to File U.S. Individual Income Tax Return) by the April 15 deadline. Remember, though, that the extension is only for the forms; you still have to pay any tax you may owe on time.

16. Not putting the proper postage on your return package. Despite the growing popularity of computer tax preparation and electronic filing, most people still do their taxes on paper forms and depend on the post office to get them to the IRS. If you are in this filing majority, don't be in such a hurry to submit your return before the deadline that you overlook the postage. Without enough stamps, the envelope will come back to you instead of going to the government. If this happens, you could end up paying a late-filing penalty (and interest if you had tax due) or spend time waiting for that much-needed refund.

Here's hoping you don't make any of these mistakes and that you get through tax season with your bank account and good humor still intact!

chapter twelve

THIS OLD HOUSE

Should You Buy?
Create a Realistic Budget for Homeownership
Make the Most of Your Mortgage

Did you—or better yet, will you—comparison shop for the best deal on your mortgage? Bankrate got some surprising responses to this question when we asked America. Despite the fact that 40 percent of homeowners refinanced their mortgages in 2004, nearly one in four did no comparison shopping to get the lowest rate. This is amazing when you consider that a mortgage is the biggest single financial transaction most people make in their lifetimes and their home the most important wealth builder.

Those who scored an "F" in financial literacy (36 percent of quiz takers) are paying almost a full point more in interest over those who scored an "A" or "B". Worse yet, in a year where mortgage rates tumbled to 46-year lows, three out of five mortgage holders did not refinance. This means they are paying more than they have to—in some cases, up to 50 percent more!

Remember the final scene in *Gone with the Wind* where Scarlett O'Hara resolves to think about her woes at Tara tomorrow, tomorrow? Her family homestead was her refuge and salvation just as our homes are for many of us. Americans regard their home as their castle. Indeed, two out of three American families now own their own homes—a record level.

However, not everyone has their eyes open when they chase the American dream of homeownership. They're the folks who think that the down payment, which typically runs from 5 to 20 percent of the purchase price, is all that they need to come up with at closing time. These people do not focus on all the other costs associated with homeownership—monthly payments, insurance, taxes, repairs, and upgrades. There is also "sweat equity," such as mowing the lawn, cleaning the gutters, painting the den, and so on. Naive, would-be homeowners think that insurance against fire, earthquakes, and thefts covers all risks. They are not focusing on the real risk, however—that the neighborhood property values will fall or the economy will worsen.

If you expect to be in a house for fewer than four years, it is likely that you will not be able to recoup the high costs of buying and selling it. These transaction fees can add up to roughly ten percent of the selling price. And in the first five years of ownership, nearly 90 percent of the money spent on monthly mortgage payments can go for interest (depending on the rate). This means that except for the mortgage interest deduction benefit, most of your mortgage payment is essentially like rent: It is money down the drain because you are not building equity. According to the National Multi Housing Council, about half of people who become homeowners move within five years. Many would have been ahead of the game had they simply rented.

There *are* tax savings to home ownership and you do build equity, but if your mortgage interest and other itemized deductions do not add up to more than the standard deduction (currently $7,200), you do not get any tax advantage.

As a homeowner, you do get the benefits of leverage—controlling the property for a down payment of only 5 to 20 percent. But on purely financial terms it may not, in fact, be a great investment. Over the long run, the value of a house is likely to rise around five percent per year, while bonds have historically returned about six percent and stocks around ten percent.

Sometimes, it's a better idea simply to rent. Although you have a limited opportunity to personalize your place, there are no tax advantages, and you're not gaining any equity when you rent, you need a much smaller amount of cash upfront. You can land maintenance-free, hassle-free living in better accommodations than your money can buy. And it is easier to pull up anchor if you relocate. According to a recent Fannie Mae survey, a third of renters said they rent out of choice, not necessity. And nearly 40 percent said that buying a home was not a priority in their lives.

Before you decide whether to rent or buy, consider how long you plan to live in the same place (if just a few years, you'll probably do better renting), how much you value the convenience of having your landlord take care of the broken dishwasher or leaky faucet, and if you can afford to buy in the neighborhood you prefer. Bankrate.com has a terrific "Rent vs. Buy" calculator that allows the user to determine their best course of action. Give it a test drive at www.Bankrate.com/rentvsbuy.

Buying a House

If you decide to buy, it is likely that you'll need a mortgage. Getting your financial house in order months before applying for one is critical. If you have any financial obligations dangling, take care of them. Start assembling your W-2s and income tax returns from the last few years, copies of pay stubs, copies of your credit reports, records of any child support or alimony, and bank statements for all checking and saving accounts for the last several months. Get prequalified or, better yet, preapproved for a mortgage. This will help you determine what kind of house you can afford, and getting preapproved could fortify your bargaining position with the seller. In prequalifying, a lender reviews—but does not verify—information about you, your income and assets, and then gives you a letter saying how much you could borrow. With preapproval, the lender verifies the information and states that you definitely could borrow a certain amount. In a case of multiple offers, wouldn't you take the sure thing? Just keep in mind that the amount for which you prequalify is the maximum sum the lender feels you can afford. This is not necessarily what you'll feel comfortable paying—or what you should opt for. Those who stretch their qualification ratios (the ratio of your total mortgage payment to your total income) beyond 28 percent (or 36 percent of their income including all their monthly debt payments) invariably wish they hadn't. They may be forced to sell, which is never a good position. Some terrific calculators to help you can be found at www.bankrate.com/Afford or www.smartmoney.com/ home/buying/index.cfm?story=howmuch. You can calculate your mortgage payment www.Bankrate.com/payment or www.smartmoney.com/ home/buying/index.cfm?story=mortgage.

Before you can make your opening offer and start the haggling (which is, after all, expected in this arena), you have to be well informed, prepared, and realistic. Learn the fair value for the home with the help of a real estate salesperson's comparable market analysis. This will show what properties like yours (or at least what you hope will be yours) have sold for recently. (Ignore those listed for sale; this is irrelevant until they snare the fox, so to speak.) You should personally check out these similar homes because condition has an awful lot to do with the price that a house ultimately fetches.

And try to find out why the seller is selling. Is he or she simply moving? Or is the seller trying to cash in on a dolt (you) in an overpriced market? One caveat: In your opening bid, do not low-ball so much that you insult the seller and torpedo negotiations.

Shopping for a home is a bit like walking through a minefield. For one thing, the friendly person who proposes to be your partner is really working for "the enemy." The agent does not represent you. He or she represents and owes complete allegiance to the seller.

If you do not want to face buying a home alone, consider a "buyer's agent." This is an agent who works only for you. Exclusive Buyer Agents (also known as EBAs) have a legal and ethical obligation to work for you, not the seller. For more info, go to www.naeba.org.

Don't wait for the "perfect" home, one that meets 100 percent of your needs and wants. It's difficult to find and while you're waiting, housing market prices are most likely climbing. Instead, experts recommend that you grab the home that meets 90 percent or more of your requirements—including those that are most important.

This doesn't mean you should reach for the stars if it means standing on your tiptoes. Too many first-time homeowners find themselves seriously "house poor" after having plunked every dime of what they earn into supporting the money pit. And if you do fall in love (or at least 90 percent in love) and contract to purchase the object of your affection, remember that there are costs to getting out of the contract. If you change your mind, you forfeit *all* the good-faith money you put down, and could face penalty clauses included in the contract.

The safeguard, of course, is the home inspection. Whatever you do, don't skimp on it. A penny wise here can be a huge pound foolish there. Make sure you and your expert check the foundation for obvious cracks or shifts, the roof for its age and overall condition, ceilings and areas around windows for leaks, and the basement or crawl space for dampness and adequate insulation. Also check the attic for the state of the structure, as well as for its general quality and workmanship; verify overall energy efficiency of the house, look for any malfunctioning electrical outlets, unusual noises, plumbing or heating problems, and check the conditions of the appliances (and whether they're included in the sale). Assess whether the exterior of the house will need repairs or paint soon, how the drainage system works, and whether there are any trees encroaching on the roof or foundation.

Today, more than two of every three states mandate that home sellers disclose known legal hindrances, physical defects and even paranormal activity relating to the property to the potential buyers. Not doing so could land unscrupulous sellers in jail—or, more likely, reverse the sale. Find out if your state abides by this mandate.

In addition to readying yourself financially, you must steel yourself emotionally. (Are you really ready to walk away from a price above your budget or expectations?) Buyers who let their emotions trump their better judgment almost always overpay.

The Mortgage Maze

Your mortgage consists of points, closing costs, and the rate you negotiate. Your lender will juggle these components to get to the profit he or she wants. You need to know when to dig in your heels and when to dig into your wallet. Knowledge is power when cutting a deal. If you have excellent credit and enough cash to make a significant down payment, then you're in the driver's seat.

When it comes to actually getting a mortgage, you must comparison shop. There are so many variables that if you accept the first plan presented, you might as well walk around with a big "kick me" sign on your back.

Comparing one mortgage to another by shopping all three major components of a loan-rates, points, *and* fees—can be tough, as some lenders give fees different names to confuse consumers. One lender might advertise that it doesn't charge an "application" fee upfront, for example. But it makes that up by charging a "commitment" fee or "doc prep" fee at closing. Other companies try to look cheaper by charging an all-inclusive "processing" fee. But they may charge $900, whereas a lender that itemizes might only charge $200 as an "application" fee, $300 as a "funding fee," and $250 as a "processing fee"—a total of $750. And lenders and brokers often quote only their fees, omitting thousands of extra dollars in other costs the borrower will have to pay.

Fixed mortgages usually come in 15-, 20-, or 30-year term increments. The goal is to shoot for the shortest term that's comfortable for you and for which you qualify because you'll save a ton in interest. If you don't qualify for or don't want to be locked into a shorter-term mortgage, experts suggest you add at least one additional payment a year, assuming there's no prepayment penalty. This will ultimately knock about eight years off a 30-year loan.

With a fixed-rate mortgage, the interest rate remains constant; you therefore know what you'll be paying for the life of the plan and can budget more easily. This dispels anxiety. However, you'll pay a higher mortgage rate initially and therefore need more income to qualify, and if interest rates go down a lot, you'll want to refinance to get a lower payment.

In an adjustable-rate mortgage (ARM), the interest rate fluctuates at specified times. The rate you pay is tied to an index, such as the Cost of Funds Index. How quickly and how much rates will move is set forth in the contract. With an ARM, you pay a lower interest rate initially (and therefore start off with a lower monthly payment) and if interest rate declines, so will your payment. It is also easier to qualify for an ARM because of the lower initial interest rate. But if interest rate increases, so will your payment, possibly making your house unaffordable.

Most "conventional" mortgages below $333,700 ($500,550 in Alaska and Hawaii) have conditions set through Fannie Mae or Freddie Mac (private corporations that are regulated by the government). Fannie Mae and Freddie Mac buy bundles of mortgages; this frees lenders to issue more loans but gives the two corporations clout over the mortgage market. Mortgages larger than the Fannie Mae and Freddie Mac mortgage limits are designated "jumbo loans" and are funded by the private investment market.

The Federal Housing Administration, a division of the U.S. Department of Housing and Urban Development, insures many low- and middle-income mortgage seekers and first-time buyers. County to county, the ceiling for the loan amount varies. In 2004, those limits were from $160,176 to $290,319.

The Veterans Administration insures (but does not fund) mortgages for those qualified by military service. No-document ("no-doc") mortgages are generally a good option for the self-employed, those who do not wish to verify their income, people with a brief or blemished credit history, and people with no credit. The application and approval processes are shorter as you don't need to provide income, employment or asset documentation. The catch is that interest rates are often higher and lenders offer them.

Many mortgage come with points—and not the kind you want. A point is one percent of the loan amount, paid in cash to the lender or the mortgage broker at closing. Closing costs can also include lender/broker fees or origination fees charged for services provided by the broker or lending institution, such as administration fees, application fees, document preparation, and loan processing fees. All are negotiable. Try to get as many waived as possible. Other closing costs are third party and government fees that the lender must pay others such as appraisals, attorney fees, flood certification, title insurance, recording fees, and taxes. While you are unlikely to get these waived, do not get gouged. Compare credit bureau fees between lenders.

Your total mortgage cost will be determined by four factors: the interest rate, fees/closing costs, the term, and the number of points. You can compare what various lenders are offering by checking out the rates posted online at Bankrate and in the real estate sections of the newspaper. Or contact the bank, mortgage company, or mortgage broker (who represents several local mortgage funds) directly. It is difficult to make sense of mortgage offers and figure out which costs are firm and which are suspect without being extremely well organized.

Some lenders charge origination points, the number of which varies with the size of the loan. Others charge administrative or lender fees or document preparation, processing, and underwriting fees. Some charge attorney and settlement fees, and fees for title searches, drawings, and title insurance; others charge for pest inspections, courier fees, flood certifications, recording fees, and state and local taxes. Most lenders estimate the cost of a title policy. A few do not, however, because they assume that the seller pays for title insurance. Find out where the bill stops when the music ends. Some lenders offer one-price packages guaranteeing the borrower will pay only a certain amount at the closing table. The best way to compare quotes is to get the good faith estimates (GFEs) and compare them side by side.

You need to know:

- the interest rate on this mortgage and exactly what you'll pay in interest over the life of the loan.
- the discount and origination points (that could lower your interest rate or provide no benefit whatsoever to you).
- the closing costs (provided via the "good faith estimate" form from the lender).

- when you can lock in the interest rate, and what it will cost you to do so.
- whether there's a prepayment penalty on this loan.
- what the minimum down payment required for this loan is.
- what the qualifying guidelines are for this particular loan (your income, employment, assets, liabilities, credit history, and so on).
- what documents you need to provide (bank statements, pay stubs, tax returns, and hazard insurance documents—or at least the name of your insurer and policy number—and verification of the last two years of your employment). If you've started a new job in the past two years, bring the contact information of your previous employer.
- how long it will take to process the application. It usually takes 60 to 90 days for a mortgage to close so make sure it covers the low rate date on which you made the deal.
- what might delay the approval of the loan.

You should also:

- ask if every fee can be waived or negotiated.
- check Bankrate.com's mortgage page for mortgage rates in your areas.
- remember that every mortgage deal is different and you must shop around. Talk to and get GFEs from four to six lenders or brokers; doing anything less could hurt your wallet.
- keep from being swindled by closely examining good faith estimates.
- seek referrals for trustworthy loan officers.
- ask a lot of questions.
- insist on getting firm, accurate estimates of all the closing costs.
- let everyone know that you will not be pushed around.

Closing Day

On closing day you must sign on the dotted line to put the title to the house in your name, verify homeowners insurance on the property, commit in writing to the terms of the mortgage, and usually, get the keys to the house. You should leave the closing as a proud new homeowner. Depending on where the closing takes place, it can include the buyers and sellers and real estate salesperson or just the buyers. It can take place at a lawyer's office or that of a title or escrow company.

Before heading to closing make sure you have a good faith estimate of closing costs from the lender, a previously secured homeowners insurance policy, and a copy of the settlement statement listing the total amount of cash you will need at closing and how it will be paid out. The statement is generally available a day or two before closing. You'll also need certified funds for closing costs and down payments. Put funds for closing costs (usually three to five percent of the mortgage amount) in reserve to pay in cash at closing.

Down the Road

If you bought your home when rates were high or have an adjustable-rate loan and want one with different terms, you might want to refinance, that is, take out a new mortgage. Think of it as walking down the aisle a second time. It's generally worthwhile if the current interest rate on your mortgage is approximately one percentage point higher than the prevailing market rate and you plan to stay in the house for at least three years. If it's not worth the costs—an application fee, appraisal fee, survey costs, homeowners insurance, attorney fees, title search and title insurance, home inspection fees, loan origination fees, mortgage insurance, and points—you might still be able to obtain all or some of the new terms you want by modifying your existing loan. Ask your lender. Most lenders sell their mortgages, so few offer modifications—they no longer own the loan you want modified.

Plan to pay an average of three to six percent of the outstanding principal in refinancing costs in a conventional loan (two to four percent in a jumbo), plus any prepayment penalties and the costs of paying off any second mortgages that may exist. Again, to help you sort through the math, there are some great free refinance calculators online. Try www.bankrate.com/refi or http://www.smartmoney.com/home/living/index.cfm?story=refin.

Whether you should refinance from an ARM to a fixed-rate mortgage requires some foresight. It all depends on where you think interest rates are—and will be. If they are really low then refinancing is wise. Also, your chances of moving come into play. If you are certain that you will be moving to a new home in five years or so, there's no point in paying extra for the 25 years of a fixed rate that you will never use.

You might also consider using the equity in your home to consolidate debt, tossing it all into a home equity loan. This does not increase your debt; it will instead shift it from various credit cards with differing due dates to one lender at a lower interest rate with a fixed repayment plan. This makes life more convenient and gives you a tax benefit, but it does reinstate credit limits on your cards and puts your home at risk if you don't pay. Experts suggest borrowing against your home only if you're adding value to it. Don't do it, if you're borrowing to finance credit cards and consolidate other loans—you're trading unsecured debt for secured debt. In other words, you're putting your house on the line.

With cash-out refinancing, a new mortgage is issued that's greater than the outstanding unpaid principal balance of the previous mortgage, letting you spend the equity you've accumulated in your homes. Unlike a home equity loan or line of credit, it's a new mortgage, not a second loan against the equity in a home.

Home equity loans are paid off over a shorter time than mortgages, which increases the monthly mortgage payments. A home equity line of credit (HELOC) is revolving credit, so you can pay off the home repairs and borrow against the line again without having to take out another loan. Since the interest on personal loans is not tax deductible and the interest expense on a mortgage or home equity loan typically is, you can save money by using the revolving credit line. A HELOC is a variable-rate loan; minimum monthly payments will not amortize the loan.

To make refinancing worthwhile, you need to lower your monthly payments by enough to cover your closing costs on the loan before you sell the house. You can refinance with no out-of-pocket costs, but you will either pay a higher interest rate than you would otherwise or wind up borrowing the closing costs. Never refinance for more than your house is worth. It makes it difficult to sell and you lose a tax advantage as the proceeds of the refinancing must go to either home improvements or the purchase of a second home to be fully deductible.

Mortgage loans on a primary residence are the least expensive form of borrowing for most consumers. Using them to pay down other debt is often wise. But people who play with this money—say, to invest in property—are betting that the property will appreciate faster than the interest expense.

The Ride Gets Bumpy

The Mortgage Bankers Association says that more than four percent of home loans were delinquent in the fourth quarter of 2003. If you're falling behind on your mortgage payments, it's crucial to act fast. This way you stand a better chance of keeping your home—or at least selling it for a fair price instead of undergoing foreclosure. Contact the mortgage company's loss mitigation department and log your calls to have a record demonstrating that you are handling the problem responsibly. Go through your budget and shed unessential items (premium cable and pricey nights out). Put the mortgage, car loan, utilities, and food and insurance bills on top of the pile, shuffling unsecured credit cards to the bottom.

Try to raise the cash and go for reinstatement: Send a check for the entire past due amount and get current automatically. You can opt for a catch-up plan where you add a certain amount each month so you catch up in a designated time. Or ask to have the past due amount moved to the back of the loan (in effect extending it a few months) or divided over the loan's remaining term, increasing the monthly payment a few dollars. Or ask the lender to reduce the rate, or offer a "silent second," in which payments on the past due amount are deferred until the house is sold.

If you fall more than three months behind without working out a deal with your lender, you'll likely face foreclosure and eviction. If you have to give up a house, there are ways to lessen the damage. Ask the lender for time and help in selling the house. If you owe more than the house is worth suggest a "short sale" in which you sell for less than the loan amount and you and the lender cut your financial losses. Or, in lieu of foreclosure, you can hand over the keys and transfer the deed to the lender, which forgives your mortgage. Then the lender sells the house. Try to avoid losing the house to foreclosure. It will severely diminish your ability to get loans at reasonable rates for years. You have some say in how things go down if the house doesn't go into foreclosure. Once it does, the lender takes the house and evicts the borrower. Foreclosure happens to those who delay too long.

The Money Pit

There's an old saying that the only things you can be sure of are death and taxes. If you're a homeowner you know there's another one: home repair costs. Many homeowners (especially new ones) underestimate the costs and fail to put aside money for this inevitability.

In addition to the visible areas crying out for attention (worn carpets, outdated kitchen, ill-fitting doors or windows), there are the invisible problems—the roof, furnace, and water heater. Ignoring small problems (such as a leaky toilet) easily can lead to big, costly ones (a rotted floor, termites, and mold, for instance).

A good rule of thumb is to put at least one percent of your home's purchase price away every year in a household fund for emergency repairs. If you paid $200,000 for your home, multiply by 0.01, then divide by 12—in this example you would put away $167 each month. As time passes, your savings will mount; if something goes wrong, you'll be ready.

Homeowners insurance typically does not cover floods, tornadoes, hurricanes, or earthquakes. If you live in an area regularly beset by any of these calamities, consider buying supplemental insurance to cover your risk. And if you own something of real value—antiques, valuable jewelry, furs, or electronics—consider buying a supplemental "rider" to kick in beyond homeowner policy limits.

Traditionally, the highest home remodeling returns have come from updating kitchens and baths. Recently, home office additions as well as upgraded amenities (light fixtures, ceiling fans, laminate floors) are also popular and may pay back a big chunk of the cost when you sell your home. A major kitchen redo cost an average of $38,769 last year, according to *Remodeling* magazine, while adding a master suite averaged $63,275. A typical exterior paint job costs $8,336. And you'll probably need more furniture, window treatments, lighting fixtures, floor coverings, and appliances through the years—all of which adds resale value to your home.

Who's Who in Buying a Home:

- An agent represents a seller in the purchase or sale of real estate.
- The appraiser visits the property to analyze the home, compares it to others in the neighborhood, and comes up with the fair market value of the property.
- The closer could be the title agent, lawyer, or someone else who prepares and presents all the appropriate documents for signatures. A normal closing generally lasts under an hour.
- A home inspector's findings are pivotal to real estate transactions. Discovering radon contamination or structural flaws, for example, could cause you to change your mind.
- A mortgage broker can be friend or foe; he or she helps you analyze your assets, match your finances with the right level loan, and negotiate mountains of paperwork. You could just as easily use a banker, although about 65 percent of home loans are originated through brokers.
- A title fee agent is the person who has searched public records to make sure the seller owns the property outright and that there are no legal obstacles to your buying it.

12 STEPS TO MONEY SUCCESS

At Bankrate, we believe that making a habit of these 12 simple steps can help everyone improve their financial well-being, for a less stressful, happier life:

The 12-Step Program for Financial Literacy

1. Keep an emergency fund.
2. Pay your bills on time.
3. Follow a monthly budget.
4. Save for retirement.
5. Read your bank account statements.
6. Get a will.
7. Shop around for insurance quotes.
8. Shop for the best credit card interest rates.
9. Check your credit report annually and repair as needed.
10. Make more than the minimum payments on credit cards. Better yet, resolve to never carry a balance.
11. Shop around for a better rate on your mortgage.
12. Adjust your W-4 form annually.

appendix
BANKRATE FORM LETTERS

Buying a Car

Negotiating a Car Lease

Auto Repair Complaint

Correcting Overdraft Protection Error

Correcting an ATM Error

Correcting a Deposit

Rectifying an Incorrect Fee

Requesting a Name Change—Bank Account

Disputing a Credit Card Charge

Disputing a Credit Card Late Fee

Requesting a Lower Credit Card Rate

Transferring Credit Card Balance and Closing the Account

Closing a Credit Card

Closing Credit Card—Lost or Stolen

Name Change—Credit Card

Opt-Out of Telephone Calls

Privacy Request

Opt-Out Direct Marketing

Requesting a Credit Report

Correcting a Credit Report

Name Change—Credit Reports

Removing Your Name from Marketing Lists

Buying a Car

Date

Name of dealership
Attention: Sales/Fleet Manager's Full Name
Address
City, state, zip code

Re: Vehicle purchase

Dear Mr. or Ms. Sales/Fleet Manager Name:

After examining various dealerships, I have decided to purchase a new or used car, the *make and model*.

I want some specific features on the car. *(In this paragraph, describe the features you would want. Include the make of the car, the year, color, and power options. Be precise. Remember: If you are not specific, the dealer will be unable to meet your requirements.)*

My research has led me to determine that I should be able to purchase this auto for *the price you are willing to pay. The dealer will work from this figure.*

I will get back to you in *number of days.* Until then, I will be contacting other dealers interested in my business. After my initial bid is selected, I will lock in financing for the auto's purchase within *number of days.*

If your dealership is interested in my offer, please be sure to include all dealer-added costs and list them according to the options that I requested. If you offer an alternative option package that would be a better value, please list it as a separate bid.

I have had no personal contact with this dealership or a specific sales representative, so this would be a "house" sale. I feel that the alternative would be unfair to other employees. Should you choose to respond to my bid with an offer, please fax the information to me at *fax number*. I will not be accepting bids after *date your offer is no longer in effect*.

Thank you for taking time to assist me with my vehicle purchase. I look forward to your prompt response and the possibility of doing business with your dealership.

> Sincerely,
> Your signature
> Your printed name
> Your mailing address
> Your phone number
> Your fax number

Negotiating a Car Lease

Date

Leasing company
Address
City, state, zip code

Re: Monthly lease payment

Dear Sir or Madam:

I am writing this letter to discuss my current automobile lease with *name of leasing company.*

I appreciate your efforts to work with me when I signed the lease on my *name of vehicle leased.* However, after I began making the monthly payments, I realized that *amount of monthly payment* is too much for my budget.

Describe in detail why you can no longer afford this particular dollar amount. Be honest, but be firm in seeking specific relief. For example: "My payment of $325 a month is not working out for me and I am requesting a new, lower payment of $275. I am willing to extend the length of the lease to accomplish this lower payment and would be happy to meet with you to discuss the specifics of making this change to our agreement."

If you decide you would rather return the vehicle and break the lease, tell the company: "I have made a decision to turn in the vehicle I am currently leasing with your company and I am willing to pay the necessary fees to make this happen. Please send me an itemized statement as to what it will cost me to terminate our agreement."

Thank you for your prompt attention to this request. I have been very satisfied with the service I have received from *name of leasing company* and look forward to working with you to adjust or cancel our current lease agreement.

> Sincerely,
> Your signature
> Your printed name
> Your mailing address
> Your phone number
> Your fax number

Auto Repair Complaint

Date

Auto repair shop or dealership
Attention: Owner or dealership service manager
Address
City, state, zip code

Re: Auto repair problem

Dear Repair Shop Owner or Dealership Service Manager:

I brought my *vehicle make and model* in for service at your establishment on *date service took place*. However, the problem is still occurring.

In this paragraph, describe the trouble that prompted you to bring the car in for service and why it is still a problem. Be as specific as possible about both the original service problem and the difficulties you continue to encounter with the auto. If you have been a regular customer and this is the first time you've had a problem with a repair, point that out. Similarly, if you've had several unsatisfactory encounters with this shop, note that, too.

I will call you on *day and time* to discuss my repair problems and to reschedule service to correct them. I also expect that the necessary work to fix my mechanical problems will be done at no further cost to me.

I look forward to working with you to resolve this repair matter.

> Sincerely,
> Your signature
> Your printed name
> Your mailing address
> Your phone number
> Your fax number

Correcting Overdraft Protection Error

Date

Name of bank
Street address
City, state, zip code

Re: Overdraft protection for account number

Dear Sir or Madam:

I am a customer with *bank name*. The name on the account is *your name* and the number is *account number*.

Upon checking my most recent statement, I discovered that my overdraft protection was not activated as it should have been.

Here, give the details of the problem. For example: "On August 10, 2003, I wrote a check (include the check number here) to ABC Property Management to pay my rent. Because my next paycheck did not come until August 15, I knew this check would be short by $150. However, my overdraft protection should have been activated to make up this shortfall. It was not, however, and my rent check bounced. In addition, I was charged a nonsufficient funds (NSF) fee for the check."

A copy of the statement with the error highlighted is enclosed for your review. *If you have documentation of when you signed up for the overdraft protection, include it.* I am also sending you a copy of my records indicating when I signed up for overdraft protection and what coverage I was told to expect from the service.

As this bank mistake caused me personal embarrassment in addition to costing me an erroneous NSF fee, I would like you to look into why my overdraft protection service did not work as it should have. Also, please remove the NSF fee from my account, implement the overdraft protection agreement as it should have been for this check, and note in your records that the incident was the bank's fault.

Thank you for your prompt attention to my request. If you have any questions, please do not hesitate to call me at *your daytime telephone number.* I will also check back with you on the status of this request and the action you have taken to rectify this bank error.

> Sincerely,
> Your signature
> Your typed name
> Your address
> City, state, and zip code

Enclosures: copy of monthly statement, copy of overdraft protection agreement

Correcting an ATM Error

Date

Name of bank
Street address
City, state, zip code

Re: ATM error in account number

Dear Sir or Madam:

I am a customer with *bank name*. The name on the account is *your name* and the number is *account number*.

Upon checking my most recent statement, I discovered an error in an ATM transaction I made last month. After reviewing my records, I am certain my most recent withdrawal was debited from my account twice.

Here, give the details of the mistake and the transaction. For example: "On August 10, 2003, I made a withdrawal of $75 from the ATM machine at 123 Main Street. This is a walk-up ATM located outside your branch at the same address. I received a printed receipt of the withdrawal, but my bank statement shows that the lone withdrawal on that date was posted to my account twice."

A copy of the statement with the error highlighted is enclosed for your review. I have also enclosed a copy of the transaction receipt that was printed by the ATM when I made the single withdrawal that day.

As this bank mistake is costing me because money was debited from my account twice, I would like you to correct my balance as soon as possible.

Thank you for your prompt attention to my request. If you have any questions, please do not hesitate to call me at *your daytime telephone number.* I will also check back with you on the status of this request and the action you have taken to rectify this bank error.

> Sincerely,
> Your signature
> Your typed name
> Your address
> City, state and zip code

Enclosures: copy of monthly statement, copy of ATM receipt

Correcting a Deposit

Date

Name of bank
Street address
City, state, and zip code

Re: Incorrect deposit in account number

Dear Sir or Madam:

I am a customer with *bank name*. The name on the account is *your name* and the number is *account number*.

Upon checking my most recent statement, I discovered an error regarding funds I deposited. After reviewing my records, I am certain that the amount in question is incorrect.

Now tell your bank the mistake you have found. Below are two examples of possible deposit mistakes.

- *I deposited $200 in my account on July 24, 2003, and my statement shows a deposit of only $20.*
- *I deposited $200 in my account on July 24, 2003, but my statement shows no deposit for that date or the next business day. (You need to check your statement for transactions the following day, too, since the time of day that you make a deposit could affect when it is posted to your account.)*

I have the receipt that I received from the teller when I made this deposit. A copy of this receipt, along with my statement that does not reflect this deposit, are enclosed for your review.

I appreciate your prompt attention to resolving this matter so that I have access to the money that I deposited on *date*. If you have any questions, please do not hesitate to call me at *your daytime telephone number*. I will also check back with you on the status of this request and the action you have taken to rectify this bank error.

> Sincerely,
> Your signature
> Your typed name
> Your address
> City, state, and zip code

Rectifying an Incorrect Fee

Date

Name of bank
Street address
City, state, and zip code

Re: Incorrect fee charged to account number

Dear Sir or Madam:

I am a customer with *bank name*. The name on the account is *your name* and the number is *account number.*

Upon checking my most recent statement, I discovered an unexpected fee for why the fee was assessed debited from my account. After reviewing my records, I am certain that the fee is an error.

Here, give the details of the mistake. For example: "On August 10, 2003, my account was assessed a $25 fee for failure to maintain a minimum balance of $500. However, my deposit records show that I had placed more than enough in my account to meet the minimum balance requirement."

Another possible fee error is a charge for using an ATM that is not in your bank's network. In this case, tell your bank: "On August 10, 2003, I made a withdrawal of $75 from the ATM machine at 123 Main Street. This is a walk-up ATM located outside your branch at the same address. I received a printed receipt of the withdrawal. Since this is an ATM operated by your bank, my transaction should be free. However, you incorrectly charged me $5 for using an out-of-network ATM."

A copy of the statement with the error highlighted is enclosed for your review. I have also enclosed copies of my deposit or withdrawal receipts, indicating the amounts and dates deposited or withdrawn.

As this bank mistake is costing me because money was incorrectly debited from my account, I would like you to correct my balance as soon as possible.

Thank you for your prompt attention to my request. If you have any questions, please do not hesitate to call me at *your daytime telephone number*. I will also check back with you on the status of this request and the action you have taken to rectify this bank error.

> Sincerely,
> Your signature
> Your typed name
> Your address
> City, state, and zip code

Enclosures: copy of monthly statement, copies of deposit or withdrawal receipts

Requesting a Name Change—Bank Account

Date

Name of bank
Street address
City, state, and zip code

Re: Request to change name on account number

Dear Sir or Madam:

I am a customer with *bank name*. My account is under my maiden name, *full maiden name*. However, I have recently married and now am legally known as *full married name*.

This letter is my formal request that you change your records of the account listed below to reflect my new legal name. In addition to my new name, your data should indicate my new address. Below I have listed the pertinent information you can use to update my bank account records:

Pre-marriage information:
Full maiden name
Social Security number
Account type
Account number
Old mailing address
City, state, and zip code

Married information:
New married name
Social Security number
Account type
Account number
New mailing address
City, state, and zip code

In addition to changing the information on my accounts, please issue me an ATM card and checks in my new name.

If you have any questions about these changes, you can contact me by mail at my new address or by telephone at *your work phone number* during business hours.

I am enclosing a copy of my marriage license. This verifies my name change and ensures accurate spelling on my updated bank records, ATM card, and checks. Thank you for your prompt attention to my request.

> Your signature
> Your typed name
> Your address
> City, state, and zip code

Enclosure: marriage license (copy)

Disputing a Credit Card Charge

Date

Billing Inquiries Department
Credit card company name
Company's address
City, state, and zip code

Re: Disputed charge on *card name, account number*

Dear Sir or Madam:

On my most recent credit card statement, which closed on *statement closing date* and which I received on *date*, there was a dollar amount charge made at *retailer name and address*. This charge, made on *date*, posted to my account on *date*.

I am disputing the charge, which is circled on the enclosed copy of my statement. I did not authorize any purchases at retailer to be charged to my account. *Elaborate on your reason for disputing the charge. For example, the product was never ordered or delivered, the product or service was not what the merchant promised, or the amount charged was incorrect.*

If you did buy the item, but the amount of the purchase is incorrect on your statement, note here that you also are enclosing a copy of the original charge slip showing the correct amount for which you should be billed.

As required by the Federal Fair and Accurate Credit Transaction Act, please adjust my account in the above-referenced amount since *repeat here why you are disputing the charge.* Please remove the dollar amount charge from my bill and notify me in writing by sending me a new statement showing the correction.

If you have any questions or concerns, please contact me by mail at the address listed below or call me at *your telephone number*. Thank you for your prompt attention to this matter.

> Respectfully yours,
> Your signature
> Your typed name
> Address
> City, state, and zip code

Disputing a Credit Card Late Fee

Date

Customer Service
Credit card company name
Company's address
City, state, and zip code

Re: Late charge on *card name, account number*

Dear Sir or Madam:

I was charged a late fee of *dollar amount* on my last bill for the above-referenced account. I believe this late fee is in error.

I received my last bill on *date*. It was postmarked *date*. The bill had a due date of *date*. I mailed my payment on date, which was in plenty of time for your company to receive and process my payment by your due date of *repeat date* shown on bill.

If you have a copy of your canceled check confirming the date you wrote it, note that here and include a copy of it with this letter. If you do not have a copy but are expecting it in your next bank statement, let the card company know that you will provide additional documentation of your bill payment timeline as soon as you receive it.

As you can see from the timetable above, I exercised reasonable and responsible judgment in paying my bill. Therefore, I am writing to ask that the fee be rescinded and the late charges removed from my bill.

If you have any questions or want to discuss this further, please contact me by phone at *your telephone number* or write me at the address below.

Thank you for your prompt attention to this matter.

>Sincerely,
>Your signature
>Your typed name
>Address
>City, state, and zip code

Requesting a Lower Credit Card Rate

Date

Customer Service Department
Credit card company name
Company's address
City, state, and zip code

Re: Request for lower interest rate on *card name, account number*

Dear Sir or Madam:

I have been a credit card holder with your company for the last *number* years. My account is in good standing and I would like to continue using it. However, I would like you to consider giving me a lower interest rate on this account.

It has come to my attention that I am currently paying *number* percent on my *name of card* while many other issuers are charging their customers far less. *Cite specific examples here (you probably get several in the mail each week), such as "I have received offers in the mail from your competitors who are offering me a lower APR if I transfer my Visa account. XYZ MasterCard charges 5 percent, while ABC Visa is offering 4.8 percent."*

I am also paying you a *dollar amount* fee each year to renew my card. I would like you to consider eliminating or reducing this fee. *Again, if you have them, give specific competing examples: "I have received offers from other companies with interest rates ranging from 0 to 2.9 percent for the first six months and no annual fee."*

In this paragraph, list additional reasons why you deserve a lower interest rate. For example: "I have paid my bills promptly, have never

incurred late charges, and have never exceeded my credit limit."
Obviously, only state what is true; your card issuer is well aware of
your credit history with the company.

For these reasons, not the least of which is my *number* years as a
loyal *card name* customer, I am requesting a lower interest rate and
asking you to waive my renewal fee. If you cannot comply, I will be
forced to cancel my card with your company and switch to a credit
card company that can give me better terms.

Please have a representative of *credit card issuer name* contact me by
phone at *telephone number* or by letter at the address below to notify
me of how much you can lower my annual interest rate and whether
my annual fee can be reduced or waived.

Thank you for your prompt attention to my requests.

> Sincerely,
> Your signature
> Your typed name
> Address
> City, state, and zip code

Transferring Credit Card Balance and Closing the Account

Date

Customer Service Department
Credit card company name
Company's address
City, state, and zip code

Re: Transferring balance of *card name*,
account number, and closing the account

Dear Sir or Madam:

This letter is my formal request to transfer the outstanding balance of *dollar amount* on my *card name* account to my following new account:

- Account issued to: *Your name*
- Account type: *MasterCard, Visa, etc.*
- Account number: *New card number*
- Expiration date: *Date*
- Issuing company: *New card issuer*

Once the transfer of my outstanding balance to *new credit card company* is complete, please close my account with your company and notify me by mail at the address below that this action has been taken. In addition, please include on my credit report that the account was closed at my own request and that the account was in good standing at the time it was closed.

If you called your credit card company earlier for guidance on closing the account, refer to that conversation now. For example: "On

May 1, 2003, I called your customer service office to discuss closure of my account. I spoke with service representative Jane Smith about the terms of closing this account and she told me that I would not be charged any transfer fees, there would be no fee for closing the account, and that you would notify me when the account was closed. Per my conversation with Ms. Smith, please confirm in writing when my account is closed and that it was done so according to the terms we discussed."

If you have any questions, you can reach me at the address below or can call me at *your telephone number*.

Thank you for your prompt attention to this matter.

> Best regards,
> Your signature
> Your typed name
> Address
> City, state, and zip code
> cc: New credit card issuer

Closing a Credit Card

Date

Customer Service
Credit card company name
Company's address
City, state, and zip code

Re: Closing account on card name account number

Dear Sir or Madam:

This letter is my official notice that I will be closing my account number by the end of the month with *name of credit card company.*

I paid the account's balance with check number *number* dated *date.* I have received confirmation from my bank that this check cleared on posting date. *If you have a copy of the canceled check or some other verification that your payment to the account was made, mention it here:"I am enclosing a copy of my canceled check to confirm that you did receive my payment. I also am enclosing my destroyed credit card."*

To my knowledge, all my fiscal responsibilities with this credit card account have been fulfilled. Therefore, please close my account and include a notation in the report to the credit bureaus that the account was "closed by request of cardholder." Once this is done, please send me written confirmation of the closure of my account, in good standing and at my request.

If there are any discrepancies between my records and yours, please contact me by mail at the address below or by phone at *your telephone number.*

Thank you for your prompt attention to this matter.

      Sincerely,

      Your signature

      Your typed name

      Address

      City, state, and zip code

Enclosures: destroyed credit card, verification of final account payment

Closing a Credit Card—Lost or Stolen

Date

Customer Service
Credit card company name
Company's address
City, state, and zip code

Re: Closing account of lost or stolen *card name, account number*

Dear Sir or Madam:

This letter is a follow-up to my telephone cancellation of my account number with *name of credit card company.*

On *date,* I spoke with *name of card company representative* to report that my credit card was lost or stolen. At that time, I told *Mr. or Ms. card representative* that I wanted this account canceled, a new card issued, and the balance from my old account transferred to my new replacement card account.

The last charge I made or authorized on this account was at *name of retailer* on *date* in the amount of *dollar amount.* Any charges subsequent to this transaction were made illegally with my lost or stolen card and should not be honored or transferred to my new card account.

I appreciate your prompt attention to my request. I look forward to receiving my new *company name* credit card and to continuing to do business with your company.

If you have any questions about my requests or the circumstances surrounding my lost or stolen card, please contact me by mail at the address below or by phone at *your telephone number.*

> Sincerely,
> Your signature
> Your typed name
> Address
> City, state, and zip code

Name Change—Credit Card

Date

Customer Service Department
Credit card company name
Company's address
City, state, and zip code

Re: Request to change name on *credit card name, account number*

Dear Sir or Madam:

My *card name* account referenced above is carried under my maiden name, *full maiden name*. However, I have recently married and now am legally known as *full married name*.

This letter is my formal request that you change your records of my credit card account to reflect my new name. In addition to my new name, your data should indicate my new address. Below I have listed the pertinent information you can use to update my *card name* account records:

Pre-marriage information:	Married information:
Full maiden name	New married name
Credit card account number	Credit card account number
Old mailing address	New mailing address
City, state, and zip code	City, state, and zip code

In addition to changing the information on my account, please issue me a new credit card in my new name. If you have any questions about these changes, you can contact me by mail at my new address or by telephone at *your telephone number*.

I am enclosing a copy of my marriage license. This verifies my name change and ensures accurate spelling on my updated account records and new credit card.

Thank you for your prompt attention to my request.

> Sincerely,
> Your signature
> Your typed name
> Address
> City, state, and zip code

Enclosure: marriage license (copy)

Opt-out of Telephone Calls

Date

Direct Marketing Association
P.O. Box 9008
Farmingdale, NY 11735-9008

To whom it may concern:

I am writing this letter to inform you of my decision to register with the Telephone Preference Service. You will find my personal information listed below.

In order to stop the calls as quickly as possible, make sure the information here is accurate: your full name, street address, apartment number, city, state, zip code, telephone number. And don't forget to sign the letter.

I would like for the cessation of telemarketing calls to take effect immediately.

Thank you for your time and prompt attention to my request.

Sincerely,
Your signature
Your printed name
Your mailing address
City, state, and zip code

Privacy Request

Date

Company name
Address
City, state, and zip code

Re: Privacy notice request

Dear Sir or Madam:

This letter is written in accordance with the Financial Services Modernization Act and the Fair and Accurate Credit Transactions Act to "opt out" of the sharing of any of my personal information in your files.

List the name on each account held with that creditor. For example, if you have a checking account, savings account, and a mortgage with one bank, list each account number and your name as shown on the accounts.

Please do not disclose personally identifiable information to third-party companies or individuals that are not affiliated with *name of bank, financial institution, or other account holder.* I also ask that you do not disclose my creditworthiness to any affiliate. Furthermore, I ask that my transaction and experience information remain confidential. Please do not send it to any company with which you are affiliated.

Thank you for respecting my privacy and honoring the choices I have made in regard to my financial information. I also would like you to please send me written confirmation that you have honored my privacy request.

> Sincerely,
> Your signature
> Your full name
> Address
> City, state, and zip code

Opt-Out Direct Marketing

Date

Equifax Credit Information Services, Inc.
P.O. Box 740241
Atlanta, GA 30374

TransUnion LLC
Consumer Disclosure Center
P.O. Box 1000
Chester, PA 19022

Experia
475 Anton Boulevard
Costa Mesa, CA 92626

Dear Sir or Madam:

In accordance with the Fair Credit Reporting Act, this letter is my formal request that *credit bureau name* remove my name from its marketing lists. I have listed below all the appropriate information to help you expedite this removal.

In this paragraph, list your full name: first, middle, and last. Along with your current mailing address also provide previous mailing addresses you've had in the last six months. Don't forget to include your date of birth and Social Security number. If you wish to explain why you want your name to be removed from the bureau's marketing list, do so here.

Thank you for your prompt attention to my request to be removed from your marketing list. Please send me written confirmation when you comply with this request.

                                        Sincerely,
                                        Your signature
                                        Your printed name
                                        Your mailing address
                                        City, state, and zip code

Requesting a Credit Report

Date

Equifax Credit Information Services Inc.
https://www.econsumer.equifax.com/consumer/forward.ehtml?
forward= home
P.O. Box 740241
Atlanta, GA 30374

TransUnion LLC
http://www.transunion.com/Personal/OrderOtherMethods.jsp
Consumer Disclosure Center
P.O. Box 1000
Chester, PA 19022

Experian
http://www.experian.com/consumer/index.html
National Consumer Assistance Center
P.O. Box 2002
Allen, TX 75013

Re: Request of credit report

Dear Sir or Madam:

In accordance with the Federal Fair and Accurate Credit Transactions
Act, I am sending this letter to request a copy of my credit report. To
expedite my request, here is my personal information:

- *Your full name*
- *Your Social Security number*
- *Your date of birth*

- *Your full address (street, city, state, zip code)*
- *Your home telephone number*

Please include all sources for the information and the complete records of any distribution of credit information to any parties by any sources.

Enclosed you will find my payment of *amount* to cover cost of the report.

If you are seeking a copy of your credit report because you were recently denied credit, mention it here. You are entitled to a free copy of your credit report if you request it within 60 days of the date that a creditor said "no" because of something in your file. Let the credit agency know that is why you want your report.

On *date*, I was declined credit by *name of creditor*. Enclosed you will find a copy of the letter from the creditor refusing me credit. Please do not share this information with any other agency.

Any other details you would like to add about the report or your credit in general should be detailed here.

Thank you for your prompt attention to my request.

> Your signature
> Your typed name
> Your address
> City, state, and zip code

Correcting a Credit Report

Date

Equifax Credit Information Services, Inc.
https://www.econsumer.equifax.com/consumer/forward.ehtml?
forward=home
P.O. Box 740241
Atlanta, GA 30374

TransUnion LLC
http://www.transunion.com/Personal/OrderOtherMethods.jsp
Consumer Disclosure Center
P.O. Box 1000
Chester, PA 19022

Experian
http://www.experian.com/consumer/index.html
National Consumer Assistance Center
P.O. Box 2002
Allen, TX 75013

Re: Credit report error

Dear Sir or Madam:

I have discovered inaccurate information on my credit report maintained by *credit agency name*. The report is in my name, *your full name* and my Social Security number is *number*.

Please find enclosed a copy of my credit report containing the mistaken data. I have highlighted the errors. Specifically, the following information is wrong:

The Fair and Accurate Credit Transaction Act defines the following as billing errors that must be corrected. Pick those that apply to your situation and detail for the credit bureau what you believe is the mistake. Be sure to list the creditor's name and account number for which the incorrect data appears.

- *A purchase made by someone other than the account's authorized user or something that you did not buy.*
- *A disagreement between the purchase price and the price shown on the bill.*
- *A charge for a product or service that was not delivered according to agreement.*
- *Mathematical errors.*
- *Questionable items or any entries for which you need more information.*

Please investigate this matter with the creditor in question; you should find there is an error. When this is confirmed, please remove this error from my credit report. In addition, please make this letter a permanent part of my credit record.

If you have any questions about my request or the credit information in question, please do not hesitate to call me at *work or home phone number*, depending upon when you would prefer to discuss the matter.

Thank you for your prompt attention to my request.

                                              Your signature
                                              Your typed name
                                              Your address
                                              City, state, and zip code

Enclosure: credit report

Name Change—Credit Reports

Date

Equifax Credit Information Services, Inc.
https://www.econsumer.equifax.com/consumer/forward.ehtml?
forward=home
P.O. Box 740241
Atlanta, GA 30374

TransUnion LLC
http://www.transunion.com/Personal/OrderOtherMethods.jsp
Consumer Disclosure Center
P.O. Box 1000
Chester, PA 19022

Experian
http://www.experian.com/consumer/index.html
National Consumer Assistance Center
P.O. Box 2002
Allen, TX 75013

Re: Request to change name on credit report

Dear Sir or Madam:

My credit information with your company current is currently held under my maiden name, *full maiden name*. However, I have recently married and now am legally known as, *full married name*.

This letter is my formal request that you change your records to reflect my new legal name. In addition to my new name, your data should indicate my new address. Below I have listed, along with my

Social Security number, my prior name and previous address and my new name and address to which my records should be changed.

Pre-marriage information: Married information:
Full maiden name   New married name
Social Security number   Social Security number
Old mailing address   New mailing address
City, state, and zip code   City, state, and zip code

If you have any questions about these changes, you can contact me by mail at my new address or by telephone at *work phone number* during business hours. I also am enclosing a copy of my marriage license. This will verify my name change and ensure accurate spelling on my updated credit report.

Thank you for your prompt attention to my request.

Your signature
Your typed name
Your address
City, state, and zip code

Enclosure: Marriage license (copy)

Removing Your Name from Marketing Lists

Date

Equifax Credit Information Services, Inc.
P.O. Box 740241
Atlanta, GA 30374

TransUnion LLC
Consumer Disclosure Center
P.O. Box 1000
Chester, PA 19022

Experian
475 Anton Boulevard
Costa Mesa, CA 92626

Dear Sir or Madam:

In accordance with the Fair Credit Reporting Act, this letter is my formal request that *credit bureau name* remove my name from its marketing lists. I have listed below all the appropriate information to help you expedite this removal.

In this paragraph, list your full name: first, middle, and last. Along with your current mailing address, also provide previous mailing addresses you've had in the last six months. Don't forget to include your date of birth and Social Security number. If you wish to explain why you want your name to be removed from the bureau's marketing list, do so here.

Thank you for your prompt attention to my request to be removed from your marketing list. Please send me written confirmation when you comply with this request.

> Sincerely,
> Your signature
> Your printed name
> Your mailing address
> City, state, and zip code

GLOSSARY

Accident and health insurance: Coverage that pays benefits in case of sickness, accidental injury, or accidental death. It sometimes provides for loss of income or debt payment if taken out in connection with a loan.

Actuary: A person who calculates statistical risks, premiums, life expectancies, and other factors for insurance firms.

Additional monthly benefit: Addendum to a disability income policy that provides an extra monthly stipend in the first year of injury, before Social Security benefits start.

Adjusted gross income (AGI): All the income you receive over the course of the year, such as wages, interest, dividends, and capital gains minus things such as contributions to a qualified IRA, some business expenses, moving costs, and alimony payments. The adjusted gross income is the first step in calculating your final federal income tax bill.

Adjuster: A person who evaluates an insurance claim and determines the amount to be paid.

Algorithm: Used in credit scoring, this complex mathematical model compares data in millions of credit reports and predicts a person's likelihood of repaying debts.

Allowable costs: Covered costs of a medical insurance plan.

Amortization: The schedule of loan payments that establishes the amount of payment to be applied to the principal and the amount to be applied to interest, usually on a monthly basis, for the full term of the loan.

Annual percentage rate (APR): The *total* interest rate of a mortgage, including the stated loan interest as well as any upfront interest (points, for example) paid in securing the loan. The APR will invariably differ from the mortgage rate quoted due to the inclusion of these items. The mortgage rate does not include origination points, discount points, and mortgage insurance, all of which are considered when computing a loan's APR. The Truth-in-Lending Act requires lenders to provide consumers with a loan's APR, which they can then use to compare loans.

Appraisal: An estimate of value of a real estate property by a professional third party. Virtually all nonowner-financed mortgages will require an appraisal; it is generally paid for by the buyer.

Arbitration: Many credit card companies require you to agree upfront to waive your right to take them to court if you have a legal dispute, requiring you instead to submit your claim to arbitration. In Arbitration, you and the credit card company would submit your dispute to an impartial, neutral third party who would settle the dispute with a ruling that binds both you and the credit card company. This arbitration decision is legally enforceable. In many cases you would have to pay for the arbitration as well. Some companies like Discover, give you 30 days to opt out of arbitration requirement, and some smaller banks or credit unions do not require it.

Assessment: The value of a property as determined by the local tax jurisdiction; it is used to determine the amount of your property taxes.

Assignment of benefits: When an insured party arranges for the plan to pay someone else directly, usually the physician or hospital.

Auto insurance score: Like a credit score, this score is based on information found in a consumer's credit file. Insurance companies consider auto insurance scores when pricing policies. Having black marks on your credit report can really bump up your auto insurance costs. Other factors that affect the cost of your auto insurance include your age, marital status, driving record, the type of car you drive and whether you live in an urban or rural area

Basic hospital expense insurance: Covers room, board, and some miscellaneous expenses for a certain number of days.

Beneficiary: One who benefits from an insurance policy, will, deed, or trust.

Binder: A temporary insurance contract that provides proof of coverage until a permanent policy can be issued.

Blanket insurance: A policy that covers common areas of a cooperative, condominium, or a neighborhood governed by a homeowners association. Such a policy does not cover individual dwellings or contents of dwellings, but areas owned in common.

Blanket medical expense policy: A plan that pays all medical expenses on a claim without limiting any services or procedures up to a certain ceiling amount.

Bodily injury liability: The part of an auto insurance policy that pays for injuries you may cause another driver or pedestrian. It includes medical expenses and loss of wages.

Buyer's agent: A real estate agent who has made an agreement to represent the buyer exclusively. This is in contrast to the agent who assists the seller and helps determine the value of a property, either for a seller or a buyer.

Capitation: A method of paying for health care services. A fixed amount per person guarantees access to specified medical services, whether plan members take advantage of them or not.

Carry-over provision: A clause in medical policy that allows a person who has submitted no medical expenses in a year to apply, or carry over, expenses occurring in the last three months of the year toward the next year's deductible.

Casualty and theft loss: A loss caused by a hurricane, earthquake, fire, flood, theft, or similar event that is sudden, unexpected, or unusual. You can deduct a portion of personal casualty or theft losses as an itemized deduction.

Catastrophic policy: A policy that typically has high deductibles and high coverage limits. Also called a major medical policy.

Charge-off: The unpaid portion of a bill that a lender understands will never be paid and has recorded on the books as a bad debt. It is a serious negative item on your credit report.

Closed access: A plan that stipulates the insured will be reimbursed for initial visits to only one doctor; this doctor must be the one to recommend more specialized care. Also known as a gatekeeper model or closed panel.

Closing: The process that effects the final transfer of the deed from the seller to the buyer and finalizes all aspects of the mortgage of the property.

Closing costs: Funds needed at the time of closing (separate from and in addition to the down payment). Loan origination fees, discount points, attorney fees, recording fees and prepaids are some items that may be included. They often will total from three to five percent of the price of the home, payable in cash.

Coinsurance: In health insurance, it is the percentage of total medical costs that you pay. If you have 80/20 percent health insurance, you would pay 20 percent of the total medical costs. Often the dollar amount is capped. For example, if you had a $2,000 cap, as soon as you spent this amount in one calendar year, your health insurance company would pay 100 percent of the medical bills after that cap is met. In property and casualty insurance, coinsurance is a provision which, in consideration for a lower insurance rate, requires you to maintain a specified amount of insurance based on the value of the property insured. For example, let's say you agree to have insurance equal to 90 percent of the value of your property and your property is worth $150,000 and you have a $30,000 loss. The insurance company pays according to the following formula: (amount agreed to pay (90 percent of $150,000), divided by the percent of the property that is covered (90 percent), times the amount of the loss ($30,000). In this case the insurance company would pay all of the loss because: the total amount the insurance company would pay is equal to ($135,000/$135,000) × ($30,000) = $30,000. If you only carry 80 percent insurance then the insurance company would pay: ($120,000/$135,000) × $30,000 = $26,667. Therefore, because you have less insurance than you agreed, you would have to come up with the extra $3,333.

Collection: A creditor's attempt to recover a past-due payment by turning the account over to a collection department. This constitutes a blemish on a credit report.

Collision: The part of an auto insurance policy that pays for car repairs after a collision with another vehicle or an object such as a fire hydrant or utility pole. It is collision insurance that makes your insurance company seek out another driver's insurance company to pay for repairs if that driver was at fault. A deductible amount applies.

Community property: Possessions, real estate, and profits that a husband and wife receive during the marriage, excluding gifts and inheritances. Upon divorce, community property is distributed equally. This legal concept is recognized in the states of Arizona, California, New Mexico, Idaho, Nevada, Texas, and Washington.

Comparable Market Analysis (CMA): A comparison of the prices of similar houses in the same general geographic area. A CMA is used to help determine the value of a property, either for a seller or a buyer.

Comprehensive: This part of an auto insurance policy covers damages to your car caused by something other than a crash. A vandal breaks in, a tree falls on it, or floodwaters engulf it, for example. A deductible amount applies.

Comprehensive major medical: A policy with a low deductible, high maximum coverage limits, and a coinsurance provision, which combines basic coverage with major medical coverage.

Condominium: Housing where the owner owns only the unit in which he or she lives—from the interior walls inward, generally—as well as a portion of the common area.

Consolidated Omnibus Budget Reconciliation Act (COBRA): Federal legislation that requires businesses of a certain size to keep former employees and their dependents on the group health plan for a limited period of time, provided the exemployee pays the premiums.

Contingencies: These are conditions or "safety valves" written into real estate offers and contracts to prevent a buyer from being forced to buy a house that is unsatisfactory, either for structural or financial reasons. Examples of contingencies are "This contract is subject to the buyer obtaining a satisfactory whole house inspection" or "Subject to the buyer being able to obtain a mortgage."

Co-pay: The portion of a bill that the insured pays, usually at the time of service. Often expressed as a set fee for a specific service.

Credit bureau (credit repository or consumer reporting agency): A clearinghouse for information on the credit rating of individuals or firms. The three largest credit bureaus in the United States are Equifax, Experian, and TransUnion.

Credit health insurance: A policy that protects a creditor should the debtor become disabled.

Credit history: A record of a person's use of credit over time.

Credit insurance: A policy that pays off the card debt should the borrower lose his or her job, die, or become disabled. The structure of protection for a revolving credit card debt is calculated each month to cover only the debt that existed at the last billing cycle.

Credit limit: The most that can be charged on a credit card or to a credit line.

Credit report: Your financial history of paying obligations (such as a mortgage, car payment, and credit cards), current balances on outstanding debts, amount of available credit, public records such as bankruptcies, and inquiries about credit from various companies.

Credit risk: The measure of your creditworthiness. Those likely to repay debts on time are better risks so lenders charge them lower interest rates to borrow money.

Credits: Tax credits are much like credits from a store. After you figure your tax bill, you can use the credit to reduce the amount of the check you must write to the government. Tax credits are more valuable than deductions because they directly cut the amount of tax owed, rather than reducing the amount of taxed income.

Debt-to-available-credit ratio: The amount of money you have in outstanding debt versus the amount of credit available on all your credit cards and credit lines. The higher your debt to available credit, the higher risk you are (and the higher interest payment your have).

Debt-to-income ratio: The ratio of a borrower's total debt as a percentage of total gross income.

Declarations page: The front page of an auto insurance policy listing the name of the insurance company, the policy number, the coverage, the cost of the coverage, and deductibles. This page also lists the vehicles insured on the policy as well as vehicle identification numbers.

Deductible: The amount that a policyholder agrees to pay toward the insurance loss. The deductible may apply to all claims made during a specified period, such as with health insurance, or to each claim for a loss occurrence, such as with automobile accidents.

Deductions: Tax deductions are expenses that the Internal Revenue Service allows you to subtract from your taxable income. If you have taxable income of $30,000 and deductions of $3,000, then you would figure how much tax you owe on $27,000. The IRS offers all filers a standard deduction amount; some other deductions such as student loan interest, moving expenses, deductible IRA contributions, and alimony payments can be found directly on the 1040A or long Form 1040. But the term is most commonly associated with the itemized deductions claimed by taxpayers who file Schedule A.

Deed: The document that, when recorded with your local government, determines ownership of a property. Transferred from seller to buyer at closing.

Default purchase rate: If you default on your account, your card issuer may sell your debt to another company or collection agency, leaving you responsible for a different (higher) rate.

Delinquent: A designation on a credit report that says you have not made the minimum payment on a loan or a credit card on time. It is usually shown on credit reports as being 30, 60, 90, or 120 days late and is a serious negative item on a credit report.

Diagnosis related groups (DRG): A system used for classification and reimbursement of inpatient hospital services.

Disability income insurance: Health insurance that provides some payment to replace lost income if the insured becomes sick or disabled.

Double-billing cycle: This term means that while the due date on your statement refers to your minimum payment, the due date to pay off your entire balance could fall earlier. Paying by the date posted on your bill could still land you with a charge for the interim period.

Dread disease policy: A policy with a high maximum limit to cover all the medical expenses associated with a particular disease.

Duplicate coverage inquiry (DCI): An inquiry by the insuring organization to determine whether an individual carries duplicate coverage.

Earnest money: The amount the buyer puts down to show that he or she is serious about the deal. He can lose this money if he backs out of the deal. It is almost always submitted at the time of the offer and remains in escrow until the time of closing, at which time it becomes part of the down payment.

Elective benefits: A lump sum that the insured can elect to take for some conditions, rather than collecting periodic reimbursements.

Entire contract clause: An addendum stipulating that everything in the insurer/insured relationship is spelled out in the contract. In other words, if it is not in writing, it doesn't exist.

Equifax: One of the three major credit-reporting agencies.

Equity: The difference between the value of a property and the total of any outstanding mortgages or loans against it.

Errors and omissions insurance: Malpractice insurance that protects architects, home inspectors, and contractors from claims by clients for professional mistakes.

Escrow: An account in which a neutral third party holds the documents and money in a real estate transfer until all conditions of a sale are met. Also, an account in which money for property taxes and insurance is held until paid; money is added to the account every time a mortgage payment is made. An escrow account usually remains in place until a borrower pays the mortgage four-fifths down. Some people are required to have them—chiefly borrowers who put less than 20 percent down and people with government-insured mortgages. Others do it by choice. Whether forced or voluntary, think of mortgage escrow as insurance for the insurance, a way for you to accumulate money for property taxes and homeowners' policy premiums (known in the business as "TI" for *taxes and insurance*) a dab at a time. (The overall monthly bill including principal, interest, taxes, and insurance is known as "PITI.")

Exemption: A deduction allowed by the IRS to help you arrive at a lower taxable income. Exemptions can be claimed for yourself, your spouse, and your dependents. The IRS allows a dollar amount for each exemption, and this amount is subtracted from your adjusted gross income to come up with the final amount upon which you must pay taxes.

Experian: One of the three major credit-reporting agencies.

Explanation of benefits (EOB): Paperwork sent by the insurer to the insured listing the cost of treatment, the charges paid by the plan, and the remainder to be paid by the individual.

Extended coverage: An addendum specifying that if the insured has an ongoing condition (like a pregnancy) that began when the policy was in force, expenses associated with the condition will be covered even after the policy has expired.

Federal Savings and Loan Insurance Corporation (FSLIC): The body that insures deposits of federally chartered savings and loan associations.

Fees: Over-limit fees are fees you pay if you charge more than the credit limit on the card. Late fees are incurred when you do not pay your bill within the present **grace period** (the number of days past the due date the credit card company will not charge you a late fee). It is important to read your bill or credit card notices to make sure that the grace period has not changed from the initial offer. For example, when you got the card you may have begun with a 28 day grace period, but, later on, your credit card company could have changed it to 20 days, making you incur a late fee if your payment is not within 20 days of the due date on your bill.

FICO score: The most commonly used credit score. The name comes from the Fair Isaac Corporation, which developed the scoring model. It is used to predict the likelihood that a person will pay his or her debts. The score uses only information from credit reports.

Fiduciary: An individual, company, or association responsible for managing someone else's assets. Fiduciaries include executors of wills and estates, trustees, receivers in bankruptcy, and those responsible for managing the finances of a minor.

Fixed rate mortgage: A mortgage loan where the interest rate is established at its origination and continues unchanged through the life of the loan.

Foreclosure: The process through which a lender takes back property from a defaulting owner and resells it.

FSBO (For Sale By Owner): Real estate that is sold without the assistance of an agent. FSBO can refer to both the individual selling the property ("They are an FSBO") or the property itself ("that house is an FSBO.")

Gap insurance: A type of insurance offered to auto lease and loan customers that owe more on a car than it is worth. Gap insurance pays the difference between what you owe and the actual cash value of a vehicle in the event the car is stolen or destroyed.

Gatekeeper model: A plan that stipulates the insured will be reimbursed for initial visits to only one doctor; this doctor must be the one to recommend more specialized care. Also known as a closed access or closed panel.

Gift card terms: If you buy something with a gift card, you may not have the same rights, like purchase protection, that you would have on a credit card.

Group insurance: Insurance coverage usually issued to an employer under a master policy for the benefit of employees.

Hard inquiry: An item on a person's credit report that indicates that someone has asked for a copy of the individual's report. Hard inquiries are requests that result from a person's applying for credit, such as a mortgage, car loan, credit card, or rental application. They are included in the formula for determining a person's credit score.

Hazard insurance: Insurance coverage that compensates for physical damage to a property from natural disasters such as fire or other hazards. Depending where a piece of property is located, lenders may also require flood insurance or policies covering windstorms (hurricanes) or earthquakes.

Health Care Financing Administration: The federal agency that oversees Medicare and Medicaid and sets certification standards for health care providers.

Health Maintenance Organization (HMO): Prepaid medical plan in which members agree to use a specific network of providers.

Home Equity Line of Credit (HELOC): A credit line you can use like a checking account. Here, however, the checks you write are against the equity in your home instead of actual money in the bank. (A home equity loan on the other hand is a fixed amount that you borrow to be paid off over a certain number of months.)

Home equity loan: Effectively a second mortgage that is second in line (after your first mortgage) to be paid off in the event of foreclosure. A home equity loan has a fixed interest rate and is amortized over its loan term so the monthly payment covers both principal and interest. Most home equity loans are taken either to make improvements that add to the value and enjoyment of the home or to refinance a good standard of living.

Homeowners' Association: An owners group, whether in a condominium, townhouse, or single family subdivision, that establishes general guidelines for the operation of the community as well as its standards.

Hospital indemnity insurance: Pays a set amount for a hospital stay based on daily, weekly, or monthly limits, regardless of expenses.

Inflation protection: Increases in benefits built into a policy to compensate for inflation.

Inside limits: Within a policy, ceilings on reimbursed benefits for certain services.

Inspection: A whole house inspection of a home being considered for purchase which looks for defects in the property.

Installment credit: A type of credit in which the monthly payment is the same every month and the loan has a set time period. The most common forms of installment credit are mortgages and car loans.

Insurance binder: A written statement that warrants that an insurance policy will be issued on a property when the title is transferred.

Interest: That portion of a mortgage payment that is the "charge" for using the lender's funds.

Itemized deductions: Expenses that can be deducted from your adjusted gross income to help you reach a smaller income amount upon which you must calculate your tax bill. Itemized deductions include medical expenses, other taxes (state, local, property), mortgage interest, charitable contributions, casualty and theft losses, unreimbursed employee expenses, and miscellaneous deductions such as gambling losses.

Judgment: A decision from a judge on a civil action or lawsuit; usually an amount of money a person is required to pay, either to satisfy a debt or as a penalty.

Lien: A legal claim against property for payment of a debt or for services rendered. One who holds a lien has the right to sell the property to obtain the money or to recover the money when the property is sold. Valid liens are filed with county recorder's office.

Listing: A property for sale by either a real estate brokerage or agent.

Living benefits rider: Provision on a life insurance policy that allows the insured to tap into the benefits to cover long-term care or expenses associated with a terminal illness.

Loan origination fee: A charge imposed by the lender, payable at closing, for processing the loan.

Loan-to-value ratio (LTV): The ratio of the amount of the mortgage as a percentage of the value of the property.

Lock-in: An agreement by the lender at the time of mortgage application or shortly thereafter to write the mortgage at a specific interest rate, whether rates rise or fall up to the date of closing. A good move if rates are rising but a bad move if they are falling, lock-ins have specific expiration dates, such as 30, 60, or 90 days in the future.

Long-term care insurance: Health insurance coverage designed to cover the cost of custodial care in nursing homes or extended care facilities.

Major hospitalization policy: A policy that typically has high deductibles and high coverage limits. Similar to major medical coverage, except that it applies only to hospitalization.

Major medical policy: A policy that typically has high deductibles and high coverage limits. Sometimes called a catastrophic policy.

Maximum allowable costs list (MAC): Slate of drugs for which the reimbursement is based on the cost of the generic equivalent.

Medicaid: A state and federal program providing some health care benefits for people who meet minimum income limits.

Medical Information Bureau (MIB): Equivalent to the credit bureau for medical information. This organization keeps health histories of people who have applied for life and health insurance and shares the information with subscribing insurers.

Medical payments coverage: This part of an auto insurance policy pays for medical expenses and lost wages to you and any passengers in your vehicle after an accident. It is also known as personal injury protection (PIP).

Medicare: Federal program that provides health benefits for people who qualify—usually those over 65 and the disabled. Medicare Part A covers hospitalization and is funded by the government. Part B, also called Supplemental Medical Insurance, covers basic medical expenses, and is paid jointly by the government and the insured.

Medicare beneficiary: Someone living below the federal poverty guidelines for whom the government is required to pick up premiums, deductibles, and copay costs for Medicare Part B (basic medical) coverage.

Modified fee-for-service: Reimbursement is based on the actual cost of services, taking into account plan limits.

Mortgage insurance: Also known as MI or PMI (for private mortgage insurance). A policy that protects the lender by paying the costs of foreclosing on a house if the borrower stops paying the loan. Although mortgage insurance protects the lender, it is paid monthly by the borrower. Mortgage insurance usually is required if the down payment is less than 20 percent of the sale price.

Multiple Listing Service (MLS): A listing (almost always computerized) of all the properties for sale by real estate brokerages in a given geographical area.

No fault insurance: If you live in a state with no fault insurance regulations, your auto insurance policy pays for your injuries no matter who was in the wrong in an accident. No fault insurance states include

Colorado, Florida, Hawaii, Kansas, Kentucky, Massachusetts, Michigan, Minnesota, New Jersey, New York, North Dakota, Pennsylvania, and Utah.

Open access: A plan that allows individuals to see another medical professional in the network without a gatekeeper referral. Also called an open panel.

Payment allocation: Your credit card payment will not pay off your highest rate balance first but you may have the right to request how your payments should be allocated. Your statement tells you this in the fine print. If you use your card for both purchases and higher-interest cash advances, or you use your card both during and after a promotional period, then it is likely you will carry charges with two different rates. Instruct the card company to pay the higher interest rate debt off first.

Permanent life insurance: Permanent life insurance is an umbrella term for insurance that lasts as long as you live (as opposed to term insurance, which lasts for a set period). Within the category of permanent life insurance are a variety of policy types, such as cash value, whole life, and universal life. It is a type of insurance that combines a death benefit, in which funds are paid to the beneficiary upon your death, with a tax-sheltered savings plan that creates an accumulating cash value. It is called permanent life insurance because the policy is open-ended and does not have to be renewed or converted, unlike term insurance, which is in force for a specified period of time. The policy offers a fixed premium but also carries significant fees.

PIP: Also known as personal injury protection or medical payments coverage. This part of an auto insurance policy pays for medical expenses and lost wages to you and any passengers in your vehicle after an accident.

Point-of-service plan: Allows an individual to choose between service from a provider in the plan network or outside of the network, with varying levels of reimbursement.

Points: Points comes from the term percentage points and refer to the number of percentage points you must pay up front for either mortgage fees or are the number of discount points you need to receive a lower rate on your mortgage. Each point equals one percent of your total mortgage amount paid at closing. Points can be "discount points" that reduce the interest rate of the loan (you are actually paying a finance charge upfront). Or, points can be origination fees, or a percentage charged for actually making the mortgage loan. When a lender, for example, quotes a rate of 8½ with 1+1 points, one point is for the origination fee and one point is for the discount fee. The two points are equal to two percent of the total loan amount paid at closing.

Preferred Provider Organization (PPO): A plan that offers discounted rates on services to members who use providers in the network. Often, if the individual seeks care outside the network, a smaller portion of the charges is reimbursed.

Premium: The amount charged for an insurance policy. A premium is based on the type and amount of coverage you choose. Other factors affecting your insurance premium include your age, marital status, your driving and credit records, the type of car you drive, and whether you live in an urban or rural area. Premiums vary by insurance company.

Prepaids: Paid for (in cash) at closing for such items as homeowners insurance for one year and real estate taxes for several months.

Prequalification: The first stage of a mortgage application where the lender will run a basic credit report and determine your debt-to-income ratio in order to see how much mortgage you qualify for.

Primary care network: The slate of primary care doctors who serve health plan members.

Principal: The amount borrowed for a mortgage loan. Your monthly mortgage payment is applied to both the interest and the principal. Be assured, though, that the majority of the payment goes to the interest portion in the first years of the loan.

Private mortgage insurance (PMI): A policy that protects the lender by paying the costs of foreclosing on a house if the borrower stops paying the loan. Although PMI protects the lender, it is paid monthly by the borrower. Private mortgage insurance usually is required if the down payment is less than 20 percent of the sale price.

Private Mortgage Insurance (PMI): Required on virtually all conventional loans with less than 20 percent down payment. Although the payments for PMI are included in your mortgage payment, it protects the lender should you default on the loan. On FHA loans, you will pay a MIP (Mortgage Insurance Premium) that accomplishes the same purpose.

Progressive taxation: The system by which higher tax rates are applied as income levels increase. The U.S. tax system uses progressive taxation with tax brackets starting at 10 percent and rising to 38.6 percent for the wealthiest taxpayers.

Property tax: An annual or semiannual tax paid to one or more governmental jurisdictions based on the amount of the property assessment. Generally paid as part of the mortgage payment.

Public record: Negative information on your credit report that has been obtained from court records, such as bankruptcies, judgments, and liens.

Rate shopping: Applying for credit with several lenders to find the best interest rate, usually for a mortgage or a car loan. If done within a short period of time, such as two weeks, it should have little impact on your credit score.

Reasonable and customary charges: Fees for medical treatment or services that fall within the average for a specific geographic location.

Recording: The act of entering deed and/or mortgage information into public record with your local government jurisdiction.

Rent loss insurance: Hazard insurance that pays for a loss in rental value or rental income if damage causes the property to become unfit for habitation.

Redlining: The illegal practice of lenders and insurance companies to deny policies, loans, and other services to people because of their ethnicity or the neighborhood in which they live.

Renter's insurance: A policy that pays for replacement of possessions but not for loss or damage to real estate.

Reverse mortgage: If you are over 62, you can get a reverse mortgage in which you borrow from your home's equity. Principal and interest are not due until you die or sell the house, but they can cost if used for only a short time.

Revolving credit: An account that requires a minimum payment each month plus interest charges on the remaining balance. As the balance declines, so does the interest charge. Credit cards are the most common form of revolving credit.

Soft inquiry: An item on a person's credit report that indicates that someone has asked for a copy of his or her report. Soft inquiries can be from current creditors reviewing the file, prospective creditors who want to send out an offer such as a preapproved credit card, or a person's own review of his or her file. These inquiries are not included in the formula for determining a person's credit score.

Standard deduction: A fixed dollar amount that is determined by one's filing status. Taking the standard deduction eliminates the need for many taxpayers to itemize actual deductions such as medical expenses, charitable contributions, or state and local taxes.

Supplemental Medical Insurance (SMI): Insurance that covers basic medical expenses and is paid jointly by the government and the insured. Also called Part B of Medicare.

Taxable income: Your overall, or gross, income reduced by all allowable adjustments, deductions, and exemptions. It is the final amount of income you use to figure out just how much tax you owe.

Third-party administrator (TPA): Company that acts as a go-between for the members of a group plan and the insuring organization.

Title insurance: Protects your title—your ownership rights—from claims against it. Paid at closing, title insurance may be the responsibility of the buyer, the seller, or both, depending on what is traditional in your locality.

Underinsured driver: This part of an auto insurance policy covers injuries to you caused by a driver without enough insurance to pay for your medical expenses. Some states include damages to your car in this coverage.

Voluntary compliance: The philosophy upon which our tax system is based: that American taxpayers voluntarily comply with the tax laws and report their income and other tax items honestly.

Waiver: The intentional and voluntary giving up of rights or claims.

Warranty: Covers either most of the items in a new home, or selected items (for example the heating and air conditioning system or the water heater) in a used home. Warranties can vary widely and are optional in used homes (paid by either the buyer or the seller).

Withholding: Also known as pay-as-you-earn taxation, the method by which taxes are taken out of your wages or other income as you earn it and before you receive your paycheck. These withheld taxes are deposited in an IRS account and you are credited for the amount when you file your return. In some cases, taxes also may be withheld from other income such as dividends and interest.

Zoning: Laws that govern specifically how a zoned area can be used. For example, an area may be zoned for single family residential, condominiums, commercial or retail, or a mix of two or more uses.

ABOUT THE AUTHOR

G. Cotter Cunningham is an authority on personal finance. For over a decade he has given consumers expert advice on their important financial matters. Mr. Cunningham is the Chief Operating Officer of Bankrate, Inc. Bankrate operates the most-visited personal finance rate information Website in the world. Mr. Cunningham and his colleagues provide consumers with comparative data and practical advice on CDs, mortgages, auto loans, banking, taxes and financial planning. Bankrate.com helps consumers to select the best financial institution for their particular needs. Bankrate provides financial data and information to a network of more than 75 partners, including Yahoo!, America Online, the Wall Street Journal, and The New York Times.

Cotter Cunningham has a unique background and perspective on personal finance. He has spent almost his entire career in finance, from working as a loan officer and running an Internet-based credit card program, to advising companies on financial strategy. Cotter believes the first step in financial independence is to foster a basic understanding of the who, what, why, where, and when of financial matters. In this book, *Your Financial Action Plan,* he provides readers with the knowledge they need to plan their financial future.

He lives in Palm Beach Gardens, Florida, with his wife and children.

For more information and advice from Bankrate, go to www. Bankrate.com

INDEX